BEYOND THE PARTITIONS

BEYOND THE PARTITIONS

QUEEN STREET STUDIOS
BELFAST

a tenth anniversary celebration
1984 -1994

DESIGN
Queen Street Studios / Crescent Arts Centre

TYPESETTING
Crescent Arts Centre

PHOTOGRAPHS
Colin McGookin and the artists
Photograph of original occupants of 37-39 Queen Street (page 8) by Robert Welch
Courtesy of the Trustees of the Ulster Museum

PRINTING
Nicholson & Bass Ltd.

ISBN 0 9523555 0 7 (HB)
ISBN 0 9523555 1 5 (PB)
British Library Cataloguing in Publication Data. A catalogue record for this book is available from the British Library.
Published by Queen Street Studios Ltd. © 1994
Queen Street Studios essay © Nuala Haughey 1994
Reasons To Be Artful © Paddy Donnelly 1994

Queen Street Studios
37-39 Queen Street
Belfast BT1 6EA
Northern Ireland
Tel (0232) 243145
Charity Registration No. X0286/94

Queen Street Studios gratefully acknowledge the support and co-operation of:
AIB Group
Arts Council of Northern Ireland
Belfast City Council
Crescent Arts Centre
Granite Properties
Harmony Hill Arts Centre
Northern Ireland Voluntary Trust

BEYOND THE PARTITIONS
QUEEN STREET STUDIOS BELFAST 1984 - 1994
a tenth anniversary celebration of an artist initiated project
a multi-venue exhibition featuring the work of past and present artists.

The Queen's Own Royal Collectives

Since the late seventies, groups of artists all over Ireland have found that by pooling their renting power and pulling on the Arts Councils' heart strings they can procure more space collectively than if they were to garret on their own.

By sharing the buildings they find, old warehouses, derelict factories, redundant offices, these artists have discovered something else: camaraderie, esprit de corps, a common purpose, to some extent, but above all a shared professionalism. Just as lawyers go to court, doctors to hospitals, engineers and architects to their sites, scientists to their laboratories, so artists must have places where they go to work too. By hanging out their shingles on the doors of these premises for all the world to see, they proclaim art as a job and a vocation for life.

In times to come, this movement will be seen as crucial in bringing the visual arts in from the periphery and putting them at the centre of Irish life. There are other factors as well of course, commissions, travel grants, purchase schemes, but the fact that so many artists have passed through such collective studios, as most of the generation of the 70s and 80s already have, will mark an epoch as important in its way as the Literary Renaissance of the turn of the century.

All of the studios that have been created are attuned to the towns and regions in which they are located: the North West Artists' Collective in Derry and Donegal, Artspace to Galway, Temple Bar Studios to Dublin, The Fire Station to that alien place called the North Inner City, Flaxart to the Shankill and the Crumlin, The National Sculpture factory to Cork, Annaghmakerrig to Monaghan and the border. These intimate entanglements are the roots that nourish the trees that have grown from these seedlings of optimism planted in cracks in the pavement or holes dug in the littered wastelands of the post-industrial age.

Queen Street Studios is now one such sturdy young oak. From its summit, if you stand gingerly on the raised bog of the roof of 37-39 Queen Street, reached by pushing up a wooden trapdoor at the top of almost vertical stairs, the Belfast Forest of Arden, the Burning Wood of Danse Inane, is laid out before you in all its sectarian verisimilitude. Charlie India Bravo British Army helicopters swoop and soar like birds of prey on the Lagan Valley thermals. The skyline bristles with observation posts. The Black Mountain, Divis, Cave Hill, the Cregagh Hills overlook the Lagan-Amazon on its meandering course among the territories of the warring tribes.

Risk walking to the edge of the red-brick precipice and you look down onto Belfast's institutions: the Tech, bastion of the old skills; the Old Museum, now a showpiece for new art; Queen Street R.U.C. Station, oddly vulnerable and unfortified from this vantage; the City Hall all florid and Florentine; and the Belfast Weather Station, Christo-wrapped for renovation the day I saw it.

That last was most surprising. Belfast weather. Surely there is no such thing? When it rains Ciaran Carson's Belfast confetti, blood, splinters of bone, gobs of flesh, eyeballs, teeth, are rain guages and anemometers not useless?

Belfast weather blows through Queen Street Studios in more than just the obvious sense that the roof leaks in downpours and water freezes in buckets in winter. This is in fact the eye of the Belfast storm. The artists who work here pluck meaning out of its swirling confusion, gather up materials let down in its wake, depict animals and people terrified by its intensity, then plot each tempest's course as it swings out into the Irish Sea, track its way across the continent of Europe, before starting to look for the next one as its towering cumulus builds over the Atlantic.

Down in the studio-weather stations themselves, the day I was there anyway, Jack Pakenham had corralled a bevy of daemons; Tim Johnson was making a memorial for vanished corncrakes; Kathy Herbert was ploughing a farm of land deep with symbols; Micky Donnelly had nailed up a pair of old doors that came in on a sirocco from the south; and Colin McGookin was furling banners tattered by the winds of history. Over other partitions there drifted the sounds of a radio tuned to the ether, water gurgling in downpipes, the rattle of hailstones on canvas, an aerial rattling against a flagpole somewhere. For one brief moment, just before I left, the honey of sunshine oozed over a damp, bulging window lintel to augur a Belfast spring, than which there is none more deserved anywhere on the island.

Just as the readings made at weather stations on Valentia Island, Malin Head, Bailie, South East Iceland and other meteorological outposts are pooled to create maps of highs and lows, occluded fronts and broken dreams, so will the work that comes from Queen Street Studios and all the other artists' observatories on the island tell us how our culture and our society fared in the closing decades of the 20th century. These haruspicators of the heavens make auguries for their times through what they paint and sculpt and build, if we just have eyes to see and ears to hear.

Such work is made of patience and method, going to the same place every day, being attentive to the changes in the climate, connecting the local with the global, seeing order in chaos and chaos in order, watching, imagining, making.

We celebrate ten years of Queen Street Studios and the work of the people who have passed through it. By their tenacity they have prevailed. This Bateau Ivre de nos jours they have created should be welcomed back from its long and difficult ocean voyage by whooping tenders, marching bands, flags and bunting, none of which the great port of Belfast should have any trouble in supplying.

Then it will be time for all the Queen's Own Royal Collectives who have sailed through uncharted waters in this glorious, valiant, leaking vessel, to drink their fill in the dockside bars and regale us with their tales.

This is the ship's log. Welcome aboard

Bernard Loughlin 1994

Queen Street Studios.
Four floors up, 68 artists and ten years on.

by Nuala Haughey

Ninety one stone stairs lead up to Queen Street Studios, a draughty fourth floor expanse of work spaces fed by labyrinthine corridors which for the past decade has been an unlikely hub of artistic activity in Belfast city centre. The number 91 is fixed in Vivien Burnside's memory since to this day there is no lift and, along with the studio's ten other founding artists, she traipsed up and down the winding stairwell for two weeks in Spring 1984 carrying materials to the top floor to construct the studio partitions.

"I remember us all measuring it up square foot by square foot and working out how much we could afford to pay," recalls Burnside. "Then we carried all the wood up those 91 stairs - 8 feet by 4 feet of hardboard sheets and 2 inch by 1 inch wooden planks - and just built it."

Formerly a printer's warehouse, the top floor space was at that time vacant, run-down and strewn with dead pigeons and pigeon faeces. When Damien Coyle - an ACE worker with the Artists' Collective of Northern Ireland (Collective) - discovered the Queen Street premises, the only commendable feature was a row of large arched windows along the length of the building's red brick facade. But after plans to take over another Bedford Street building fell through, the Queen Street site became, by default, the first ever large-scale artists run studio scheme in Northern Ireland.

"As far as studio provision at the time went, it was quite good," says Coyle. "It was quite innovative. I think it was actually a big sea-change for the visual arts in Northern Ireland. It showed that artists could take control, they could do something for themselves."

With a £3,000 Arts Council start-up grant and a reduced rent from a sympathetic and supportive landlord, the partitioning of the floor space began, with artists apportioned as much square footage as they could afford to pay for. "It was quite territorial," Coyle laughs. "I must have done about ten variations on floor plans with negotiations as we went along. It was like Bosnia-Hercegovina."

But the dimensions of the transformation of the visual art scene in Belfast that this bunch of enthused and idealistic artists helped initiate in the early 1980s have, more than a decade on, extended far beyond the modest geographical boundaries of the studios. The initial momentum for the establishment of artist run studios which led to Queen Street being set up came from the

Collective. Its formation was in turn initiated by Art and Research Exchange (ARE), a Belfast-based charity providing art facilities for artists and the community which was inspired and grant-aided by a visit to Belfast in 1977 by the now deceased German artist and activist, Joseph Beuys. A co-founder of the Free International University - a network of cultural workers committed to creativity across traditional class and cultural boundaries - Beuys' Belfast trip led to the formation of the Northern Ireland Workshop of the Free International University which was soon renamed ARE.

And it was ARE which in May 1981 distributed a large poster around Belfast asking artists: "Do you really have a future in art?" and urging them to attend a meeting on the future of the visual arts in the north. The agenda of that vigorous meeting in ARE's Lombard Street offices on 28 May 1981 - the formation of an

artists' collective in Northern Ireland - was overwhelmingly supported by the 100 students, graduates and college lecturers in attendance. The Artists Collective of Northern Ireland was promptly formed in June 1981 with a remit "to act on one hand, as a forum for greater communication and provision of resources for artists and, on the other hand, to act as a lobbying body to present the views of its members to funding authorities and institutions".

Perceived as a long overdue unionisation of visual arts, the Collective was, in line with its egalitarian Beuysian roots, open to artists as well as "interested persons". Coyle remembers that first night's meeting as a lively brain-storming session in which ideas were bandied about and frustrations with the status quo aired.

He recalls: "There was quite a lot of hostility towards the Arts Council. Everybody felt that it wasn't providing the service they wanted. They wanted a better format for the distribution of Arts Council funds. As well as that there was no studio provision, no real gallery accessibility for unestablished artists and no good arts suppliers in Belfast."

In Belfast at that time the only art galleries were the Arts Council Gallery in Bedford Street, the Bell Gallery in Adelaide Park, Tom Caldwell in Bradbury Place and the Octagon in Lower Crescent. All, with the exception of the Octagon which was largely a print gallery, showed work by artists described euphemistically by one fine art lecturer as, at the very least, "middle order artists". Certainly the only gallery at the time providing exhibition opportunities for recent graduates was that run by ARE in its Lombard Street premises.

Knowledge of availability of grants and funding opportunities was not easy to come by and artists perceived the Arts Council as a prepossessed Wizard of Oz-like body dispensing funds but little information. Una Walker, Collective chairwoman for two years, remembers life for artists before its formation as grim. "Really when we were at college there was no back-up and no kind of indication that we would ever work as professional artists here," she explains.

"You went through the fine art course and you didn't really know artists and there were very few artists working. The sort of things being shown in the Arts Council Gallery were touring shows of very established

people and it wasn't a particularly welcoming place either. So you didn't actually come across the idea that you would be a working artist. It had been a totally closed world but what has changed since then is the whole notion that people would actually work as professional artists - that people learned to have some kind of a commitment."

And it was the commitment of Walker's contemporaries - art graduates, students and practising artists - who attended the monthly Collective meetings determined to turn that notion into a reality.

"I think, basically, the formation of the Collective was the beginning of really quite a strong impetus and quite a significant growth and profile for young and middle career artists who had been having difficulties," says Alastair Wilson, a fine art lecturer in the University of Ulster's Faculty of Art and Design, who attended early Collective gatherings.

"It did seem to me to be a turning point because there are now a great number of young artists working and when they come out of college they now know there is a group of like-minded people out there who have been through a lot of the problems that they're going through."

The Collective drew up an ambitious and high-minded policy document defining its agenda as: education, information, lobbying for tax reform, persuading the Arts Council to establish a permanent New Contemporaries show in the north and facilitate the setting up of accountancy services for artists, the development of links with industry and distinct recognition for Northern Ireland artists in the International Association of Artists.

A publications committee was set up which launched Circa, an independent art magazine, in November 1981. In 1983 Circa increased its funding from the northern and southern Arts Councils, which paid for a part-time administrator. Circa is currently the only publication devoted exclusively to contemporary visual culture in Ireland.

The Collective also set about organising exhibitions for its initial 100 members in an effort to provide "a more stimulating climate for the visual artist in Northern Ireland" and to democratise the visual arts by providing outlets for artists to exhibit their work to as wide a public as possible.

Maysfield Leisure Centre in east Belfast, Andersonstown Leisure Centre in west Belfast and Queen's University in south Belfast were three Collective exhibition venues in 1981 and 1982 and two Collective artists had temporary studio residencies in Maysfield Leisure Centre.

Within a year, the Collective made contact with institutions, obtaining access for members to seminars and the free use of library facilities in the Art and Design Centre, Belfast, a contract for bulk purchase of art materials by mail and discount arrangements at various arts suppliers.

In 1983, the Collective's open decision-making system was disbanded and replaced by a single management committee, with Walker as chairwoman. A shift in emphasis towards a more centralised organisation to act as a contact point for artists and facilitate the exchange of information was achieved by the appointment of Coyle as Collective administrator in the same year.

When he took up his post, Coyle recalls being given a telephone and a desk in the ARE offices. "I didn't have any brief at all," he says. "I had to create the job for myself." His first task was to compile a questionnaire which he distributed to the Collective's 100 members. The returned forms showed that artists' priorities at the time were affordable studio spaces and an information newsletter.

Coyle viewed around ten city centre sites in search of suitable and affordable studio premises before "stumbling upon" Queen Street. Given his lack of business experience, the task was, Coyle admits, "quite hairy" and confirmed his hunch that "all landlords are difficult".

He says: "I wonder about the fact that it got off the ground at all. When you think about it, you got eleven people giving up their free time to haul bags of plaster and stuff up those stairs to build studio space. There is a certain naivety about that and a certain innocence. But I think that whole experience of doing that, building the spaces, created a big bond between those people that still exists to this day."

The studio members' November 1984 debut show, Collective Images, was housed in the building's temporarily vacant ground floor shop unit with a poster in the window announcing it as a new city centre gallery.

The early annual open days - still a regular highlight of the studios' calendar - attracted schools groups and media attention, with Queen Street Studios' artists becoming the obliging subjects of countless 'O' and 'A' Level tracts.

In 1984, a three months free studio residency scheme for recent fine art graduates was also set up in an effort to foster links with the Art College and this continued for two years. An expansion in 1984 added another five work spaces and was followed in 1985 by a further extension which created four more spaces, although the level of Arts Council funding did not increase proportionately.

Despite annual Arts Council funding applications in the region of £20,000 to £30,000, Queen Street Studios survived on annual budgets of between £2,000 and £5,000 for the first six years. But what the studios and the Collective lacked in financial support was compensated for by the vigour of their members.

By 1986, a slide library of members' work was in place and Arts Council guests and visiting curators were regularly brought to see the work of Studio residents. Collective membership at that time included a membership card which entitled the holder to access to the Art College library, lectures and seminars held in the college, a 10 per cent discount on artists supplies in selected outlets, special Circa subscription rates and invites to Collective social events.

The newsheets from the period - cheerfully crude photocopies on folded A3 sheets - contained updates on the work of the Collective, open submission exhibitions, awards, exhibition listings, ongoing campaigns, art events and parties. "There was always something going on", says Coyle. "Every month we had some sort of activity." They included lecture series or slide talks by studio tenants or invited guests.

Because Queen Street Studios housed the Collective's administrative office, they quickly became its public face. Collective members regularly exhibited work in the studios, including the successful open submission post-card exhibition in July 1985 which toured Britain and Ireland. Other Collective exhibition venues included the Corridor and Peacock Galleries in Lurgan in 1985 and 1987 and Harmony Hill Arts Centre in Lambeg in 1986. The Harmony Hill exhibition of work by 47 of the then 80 Collective members, Collective Images, was heralded in the Irish News by Brian McAvera as a display of "what's happening in art at the moment". He wrote: "Most of the interesting painters and sculptors in the north belong to the Collective. Galleries from Fenderesky's to the Crescent, from the Peacock to the Otter would be much poorer without Collective members who span the generations."

For the Collective's younger artists, the traffic of ideas and experiences facilitated by the diverse membership was also enriching. "I suppose, artistically and formally, we didn't have a great deal in common," admits Burnside. "But we were so interested to see what other people were doing. It was great mixing ages and getting peoples' very different experiences. From the ad-hocness of the shows, the vigour and excitement of people came across in them." With Queen Street tenancies still available on a first-come-first-served basis, age and ability range continues to be a vital and valued characteristic of Queen Street Studios.

Tim Johnson has had a sub-let studio in Queen Street since September 1993 and he states with disarming sincerity that it has changed his life. "I feel now like I'm part of an artistic community," he says. "On the open day I made contacts plus there's always an awareness of grants and things through word of mouth. Some of the people here have been in the business a lot longer than me and at meetings that really increases the total experience of the group."

According to Alastair Wilson, the mixed abilities and ages of Queen Street's residents is a "plus factor" and he strongly dismisses claims by former Art College students that the teaching fraternity there looks down on students joining the artistic medley that is Queen Street. He says: "Its function is not to provide a united front as a collective of people all working the same way. It is a group of individual people who actually need a situation to work and perhaps the comfort and the encouragement of like-minded beings in the same situation. It becomes sort of multi-principle, multi-media, multi-everything. It becomes, if you like, probably much closer to society generally, warts 'n' all."

The Collective's warts began to appear in 1987 when its Action for Community Employment funding from the Department of Economic Development for a full-time administrator was suddenly cut. The post's then incumbent, Paul Finnegan, started working part-time, his puny allowance provided out of the already over-stretched studio budget of £3,000. "I couldn't believe that ACE posts were being handed out to various other groups," says former management committee member Colin McGookin. "It seemed to be either public sector, church, or community groups with politicians behind them that got these posts and people like ourselves who were well educated but didn't have a lobbying side to us were never able to get them."

The loss of funding for the administrator's post - a keystone of the Collective and a focal point for the studios - signalled a down-turn in Queen Street's activities and morale. The September 1987 newsheet had a quirky front-page drawing of two dancing figures advertising the forthcoming Collective party, but the inside report on the June open meeting was sombre. At that gathering it had been agreed that the administrative workload of the Collective and the studios should be redistributed among studio members to absorb the loss of the ACE funding. The management committee also felt the need to "re-establish and up-date" the long term policy of the Collective "in order that, in the future, management can better direct its efforts to achieve collective goals".

A revolving three member studio committee was set up to co-ordinate studio activities and organise meetings, with a representative reporting to the management committee on the progress of the studio committee.

Seven sub-committees were also formed, chaired by management committee members. Their remits were: an education programme, events/exhibitions, studio open day, artists in industry, newsheet and galleries/contracts with shared responsibility for fund raising. Believing the public profile of the Collective to be too low key, it was agreed that the thrust of future policy was to be INVOLVEMENT (original emphasis) by the membership in Collective projects and in the wider community.

"It was felt that more public awareness was necessary to encourage support and recognition for the Collective both as an organisation and as individual artists," states the news sheet.

In an initial surge of activity, community centre workshops were organised, efforts were made to co-ordinate the members' slide library and an ambitious new arts week programme with outreach events was planned. Links were forged with studio groups in the Republic of Ireland and Britain, with Queen Street hosting a rotating committee meeting which included the British National Artists Association, the Association of Artists and Designers in Wales, and the Association of Artists in Ireland. But in practice, most of these efforts fell far short of the exuberance of the news sheet's future policy brief.

"All those things were too big for us to handle," admits McGookin, who was charged with organising events and exhibitions. "We used to make initial contact with these groups and they were interested enough but our follow on was never there. We really needed an administrator to follow up on a more committed level."

For the next three years, Collective and studio administrative chores rested with Finnegan and the studio committees. This situation caused antagonism among the voluntary committee members who felt their artwork was taking second place to the administrative demands of the Collective. Collective group exhibitions were a particular source of frustration, with studio members having to take responsibility for the work submitted by the Collective members.

Despite the 1985 expansion which almost doubled the studios' size, the annual Arts Council grant never climbed above £4,000 during this period and this financial glass ceiling inhibited the work of the studios and the Collective.

According to former tenant and management committee member, Mark Pepper, the consistent lack of Arts Council financial support for the Collective throughout the 1980s is attributable to its ambivalence as to whether it was within its remit to fund an artists-run studio group and a lobbying body like the Collective.

"They were definitely not interested in the idea of funding a Collective - that is a lobbying body," says Pepper. "They thought we were trying to muscle in on their territory in some way."

But the Arts Council's then Visual Arts Director, Brian Ferran, dismisses this claim. Citing as an example the lack of Arts Council funding for the National Campaign for the Arts which the UK Arts Councils associate with, he stresses that it is not the Arts Council policy to fund lobbying bodies.

He says: "The grant was for the studios. The Arts Council gives in the main, almost exclusively, grant aid for specific projects, not to sustain organisations. The greater need felt by the Arts Council was for the studios rather than sustaining an organisation."

As early as 1988, a proposal to disassociate from the Collective was circulated among Queen Street Studios' members. The Northern Ireland Council for Voluntary Action suggested a new draft constitution for the studios, advising them to re-define themselves as a community-based education group in order to attract more funding.

"There was a feeling that the studios should reconstitute themselves as a studio based group without all the baggage of the Collective, without all those high ideals but with more business-like proposals for going forward," says McGookin.

This proposal was circulated among studio members but was never acted upon. Then, in June 1989, McGookin received a phone call informing him that the studios were listed in Stubbs Gazette business information magazine for non-payment of £1,431.35 in rates.

A four person emergency committee was set up and the debt was cleared but this crisis brought other problems to the attention of the management committee. Due to general maladministration and lethargy, some studios had been left vacant and rents and other bills had not been paid on time. For a studio group run on a shoe-string budget, it didn't take long to snap.

"I just see it as part of the malaise that had set in, part of the inertia," remarks McGookin. "Everything had just slowed down to the point of just ticking over and nobody had any sort of ideals any more - they had all gone by the wayside and the studios were seen as part of the furniture. Recent graduates would come in and use the place and leave again and nobody knew who they were. You felt like you'd had the stuffing kicked out of you over the years. The grant was so low, there was nothing really exciting going on, there was no money to do anything with. There may have been ideas around to do something but there was no incentive to make applications because all the applications seemed to be hitting against a brick wall."

The emergency management committee was faced with the choice of closing the studios or, recalls Pepper with a chuckle, "doing something a bit more radical" - which was to expand and try to bring in more capital to swallow some of the previous debts.

The step taken was the more radical one, with another eight studios created by the extension into the neighbouring top floor space. The newsheet was also up-graded and further short-lived attempts at a community education programme initiated. But despite expanding to 7,720 square feet, the Arts Council grant to Queen Street Studios increased by only £1,000 to £5,000 for 1990/91. In real terms, this was actually a substantial reduction in funding.

By 1990, the initial communal fervour of 1981 had reached a natural plateau and attempts to maintain the studios and the Collective in tandem succeeded only in dissipating the energies of the artists themselves and both groups.

In the same year as the Queen Street expansion, Flaxart studios on the Crumlin Road, north Belfast, were set up by five recent fine art graduates.

Founding Flaxart member and former Queen Street tenant, Michael Minnis, recalls that there wasn't a place where sculptors or mixed media artists could work on a large scale. He says: "That sort of work wouldn't have been appropriate for Queen Street. There was a sense that another place was needed where larger scale work or sculptural work could be done. That's how it started off, as a group of people who wanted to get together because we were interested in each other's work and in sympathy with each other."

Flaxart's formation provided an impetus for the Queen Street management committee to get the studios running smoothly again by chopping off the dead wood of the Collective.

In Spring 1991, the tenth anniversary of the Collective, an open meeting was called at which its future was the main topic of debate. At that meeting, members acknowledged that many of the Collective's original aims had been met.

Circa was well established as a source of debate and information for artists. Belfast had many galleries providing exhibition opportunities for young artists, including On The Wall (later the Kerlin Gallery), Fenderesky, the Otter, Queen's Common Room and the Crescent Arts Centre. Several other small studio groups had sprung up in Belfast city centre and the Collective had forged links with other studio groups through the Dublin-based Artists Collectives and Group Studios in Ireland, and the Association of Artists in Ireland.

But Collective membership had dropped off to about 30 and the annual exhibitions became a chore for the studio residents charged with hanging and sometimes even mounting the work. By unanimous vote then, it was agreed at that meeting to wind up the Collective with the recommendation that if a lobbying body wanted to reconstitute itself, it should do so independently of Queen Street Studios.

On the demise of the Collective, Walker, currently an executive committee member of the 600-strong Association of Artists in Ireland, the Republic's main advice and lobby group for artists, refers to what she calls the "critical mass theory".

She says: "I don't know whether there has ever been enough people who will actually start something going and keep it going for the required period of time. I don't know whether it's a case of the north of Ireland being such a small place. I'm not so sure how far the lack of any kind of effective political structures here has affected peoples' ability to work politically - to actually understand the processes - but I do think that has something to do with it and the lack of effective politics means that very frequently people are incapable of concentrating on issues and always reduce themselves to personalities."

The Collective had never made much headway in its lobbying aims despite its contacts with the AAI, which functions as the Irish National Committee of the International Association of Art (IAA). While a northern branch of AAI was formed in 1990, it never gained momentum because, says McGookin, many northern artists viewed the AAI as impotent in dealing with their legal problems.

Whereas the AAI has succeeded in directly lobbying politicians on artists' issues in the Republic and has a European regional committee, it has no muscle in the UK's Westminster parliament.

Westminster rule means that artists in Northern Ireland have no direct access to the law makers and the political impotence of local councillors is amplified by the 'troubles' which create a scale of priorities among which artists' demands for reforms to the social welfare system do not figure highly.

"In a way, maybe the exhibition programmes and the setting up of the studios was all that could realistically be achieved by the Collective at that time," says founding Queen Street member Ann Carlisle. "Those were really terrific achievements in themselves with not a lot of money."

From 1991 onwards, Arts Council funding applications were drafted purely for the studio provision - and the funds more than doubled in 1991/1992 to £12,000 with £11,000 for 1993/94 and £12,000 for 1994/95.

Ferran maintains that the 1991/92 grant increase was in no way connected to the dissolution of the Collective. While acknowledging that conditions at Queen Street are not ideal, he says every Arts Council client claims to be underfunded and that it is the Arts Council's responsibility to keep as many enterprises as possible afloat with the resources available.

He says: "The Arts Council support system is governed by the amount of money given by the Department of Education and if there are all of these projects demanding survival then the only way in which new projects can be allowed to enter the field is with whatever increase the Arts Council gets from year to year and we go along very frequently on the basis of a leap-frog system where an enterprise is kept ticking over and as long as it survives we are perfectly happy and if there is the opportunity to allow it to thrive a little either by a windfall of money or the falling out of some other enterprise, then we do that."

But even on the Arts Council's 1994/95 grant of £12,000, Queen Street Studios are today persevering rather than thriving on basic annual running costs of around £19,000 (including rents, rates, service charges and insurance).

Conditions in the building are deteriorating with some of its 22 studios made almost unusable by the spontaneous roof leaks and poorly insulated windows and ceilings. Although the bone-chilling concrete floors in some of the studios have been covered with wooden panels, for certain winter periods many of Queen Street's 24 current artists simply stay at home to work rather than spend their days hunched over a gas heater trying to warm their fingers sufficiently to allow them to work.

On a drizzly winter morning in February 1994, five of the studios' artists are huddled in the communal space clutching their coffee mugs for warmth while the heater struggles feebly to make an impression on the cold atmosphere. These artists agree that, given the reasonable rents in Queen Street Studios of between £20 and £40 per month, the conditions are "not bad".

"Most artists are used to working in these sorts of conditions without central heating or whatever," says Colette Lee, a studio tenant for the past three years. "Nobody else would be expected to work in these sorts of conditions but we do."

But should artists have to? Compared with funding by the Republic's Arts Council (An Chomhairle Ealaíon), the budget allocation for studios by the Northern Ireland Arts Council is far below par. Out of a total 1993/94 visual arts budget of £839,000, An Chomhairle Ealaíon allocated £230,800 to funding twenty-seven studio groups throughout the country. This amount includes £31,000 for Graphic Studios, £50,000 for Temple Bar Studios and £55,000 for Fire Station Studios, all in Dublin.

In the north in the same year, out of a visual arts budget of £807,345, only £19,000 was channelled into studio provision - £12,000 for Queen Street Studios, £3,000 for Flaxart and £4,000 for the Derry-based North-West Artists' Association which provides nine studio spaces.

For 1994/95, the budget has increased to £25,300 with £2,800 going towards basic sanitation facilities to Carlisle Circus Studios, based in a disused church in north Belfast, and £1,000 for lights and equipment for Magpie Studios in King Street. Queen Street Studios received £12,000, Flaxart £5,000 and the North-West Artists' Association £4,500.

According to the Arts Council of Northern Ireland's Visual Arts Director (acting), Noírín McKinney, funding for studio provision is "something that's always high on our agenda and what we've done so far is to try to respond to need as far as possible. If capital resources were to become available, certainly the provision of a much better standard of studio spaces would be something that we would be thinking about."

With the level of government funding for the Arts Council of Northern Ireland still lagging far behind other UK regions, additional capital resources are likely to come from the anticipated annual Arts Council boost of £1.5m to £2m from the national lottery as of 1995.

The paradigm of studio provision in Ireland is Dublin's Fire Station Studios, a residential and workshop facility for practising artists on the city's northside which accommodates ten live-in artists as well as sculpture workshop facilities.

Set up two years ago as an Arts Council initiative, and also funded by Dublin Corporation, the studios are currently running a European funded Horizon Programme which provides £200,000 over two years to train eight local long-term unemployed people in technical skills of assistance to sculptors. Fire Station Studios' director Robert McDonald says: "The set-up here is unique in that it's residential and has a community or social remit as well as providing a broad range of services for practising artists so we're not a stand-alone set up. We engage with the community and have a social and cultural role."

McKinney acknowledges that the Fire Station scheme would "certainly be a good model if it proves to be highly successful and something that a lot of artists were benefitting from". But she insists that artists have yet to show a strong enough demand for such facilities in the north. "It hasn't come out clearly as a demonstrated need which we would consider seriously," she says.

"Due to the fact that we haven't whinged and moaned about it, we probably haven't demonstrated a need because we are so happy to get anything in this city," says McGookin. "If you even get a leaky old building you feel like you've got something good. We don't think big in this city and it's because nobody has ever been encouraged to think big by being rewarded for doing so."

But Queen Street Studios have been rewarded for doing just that - with a £25,000 AIB Group Better Ireland Award in the 1993/94 arts/culture category. Exhibitions, workshops and lectures are programmed for 1994 (Queen Street Studios Tenth Anniversary year) in an attempt to raise the profile of the studios with both the public and policy makers.

"I think the tenth anniversary project will show where the need is." says McGookin. "This is our attempt to show what we need on the ground, what we've achieved on very little and what we could possibly achieve with more. We're trying to show what our experiences have been and where they point to for the future."

In January 1994, Belfast City Council appointed a new Arts Officer, Chris Bailey, whose remit is to overhaul arts policy. Bailey pledges to pursue a more "pro-active" funding policy towards visual arts out of the Council's annual £1/4m arts budget. While this new determination will hopefully lead to increased funding opportunities for visual artists on an individual and group basis, a capital injection from City Hall for Queen Street Studios is unlikely. Given that the City Council already provides revenue funding to the Ulster Orchestra, the Civic Arts Theatre and the leisure centres as well, Bailey opines that there would be a "reticence to become involved in a different discipline".

Queen Street Studios' tenth anniversary management committee is aware that, having at last achieved charitable status, future funding from industry, private sponsorship and European sources must be explored. To facilitate this, funding is needed for a core-worker in the studios, but successive annual Arts Council applications for an arts worker's salary have never been successful. The climate in which Queen Street Studios are currently vying for financial backing is radically different from that which existed a decade ago.

Numerous small studio spaces have burgeoned in Belfast. An effective, if informal, support and communications network among the 80 professional artists in the Belfast area is well established, with visual artists accounting for 71 per cent of Arts Council applications for awards, bursaries and fellowships in 1993/94. The quantity (if not the quality) of exhibition opportunities is acknowledged by artists to be better than many cities of a commensurate size in the rest of the UK.

The aims of Belfast-based artist run groups now, such as Catalyst Arts, 6 Into 18 and Ad Hoc, are to initiate and secure funding for international exchanges and exhibitions in non-art venues throughout Belfast. With a consensus among artists that there is yet a need for a pressure group to replace the Collective, Ad Hoc, which represents 60 artists, may be the most appropriate vehicle for such an initiative. If the palette these groups are working from - renewed calls for a lobbying body, social security law reforms, a raising of living standards and recognition of artists professional status - is similar to that of the Collective, then the canvas has at least been primed by the efforts of their predecessors.

"There's a far more solid base here now to work on than ever," says McGookin. "We've built strong foundations. Ten years ago there was very little going on and we were just trying to set up a back-up support, a body of people who were trying to change things. It's certainly a more healthy and confident environment now than then."

And artists are today confident that the next decade will be at least as successful as the last. "Northern Ireland is beginning to come out from under the stone which has flattened it for the past 20 years," says Queen Street tenant, Kathy Herbert. "The rising tide lifts all boats and art is going to be no exception and the fact that people are getting together in new groups is a sign of it."

And echoing the words of another Northern Irish success story, the chart-topping Derry band D-Ream, Herbert adds: "Things are definitely moving in the art scene. Things can only get better."

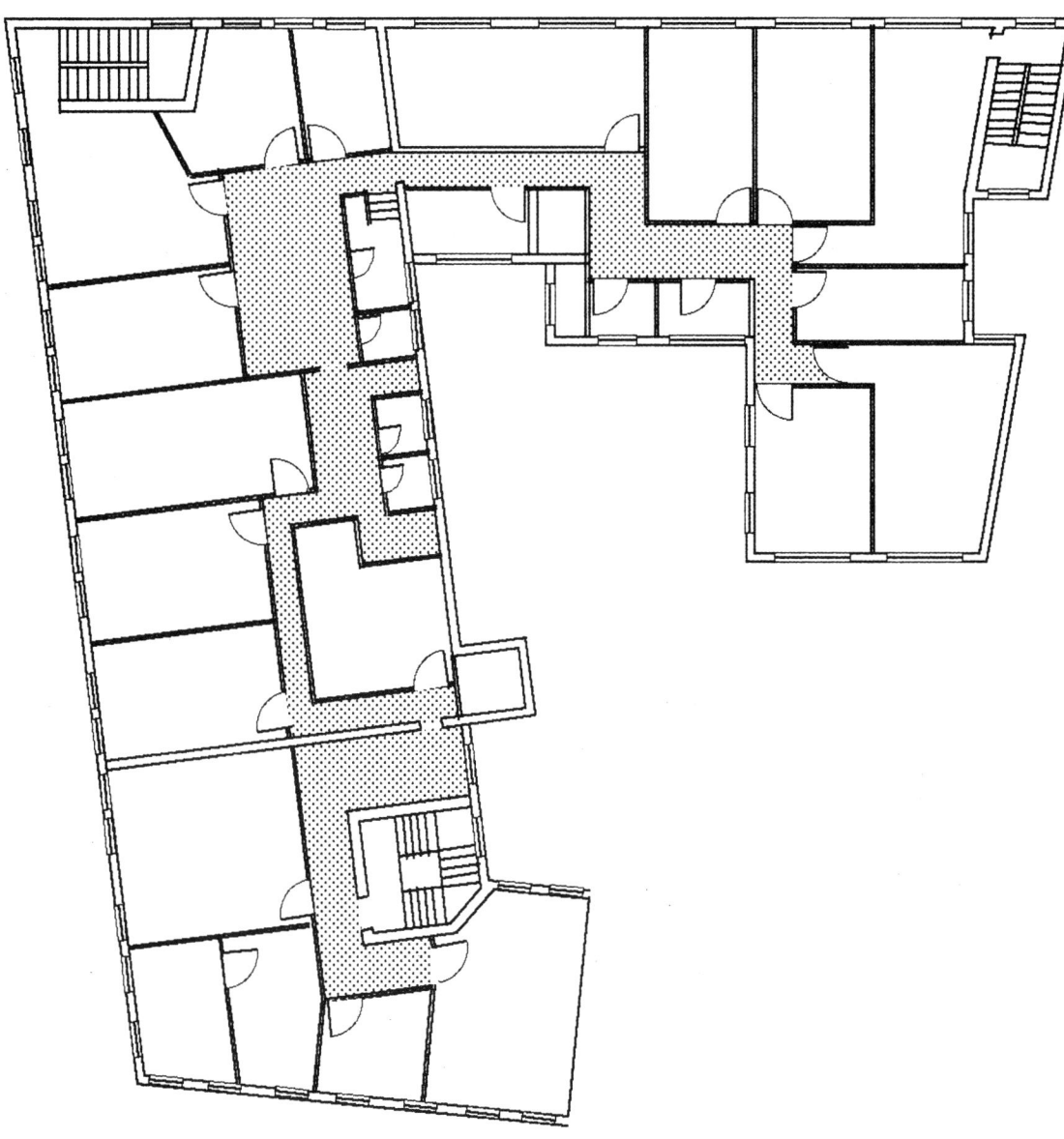

Layout of Queen Street Studios - 21 partitioned spaces. Scale 1/250.

QUEEN STREET STUDIOS ARTISTS 1984 - 1994

Anthony Bartley
Cliff Brookes
Una Bryce
Vivien Burnside
Lorraine Burrell
Elaine Callen
Anne Carlisle
Lucy Cheyne
Anne Clarke
Brian Connolly
Damien Coyle
Mary Ann Curren
Marie Therese Davis
Gerry Devlin
Moira Doherty
Micky Donnelly
Brendan Ellis
Frank Eyre
James Fearon
Paul Finnegan
Philip Flannagan
George Fleming
Nora Gaston
Gerry Gleason
Nuala Gregory
Ian Hamilton
John Hamilton
Kathy Herbert
Frank Holmes
Ronnie Hughes
Tim Johnson
Brendan Kelly
Barbara Lavery
Colette Lee
Terry McAllister
Denis McBride
Damien McDonagh
Colin McGookin
Jim McKevitt
John Mathers
Michael Minnis
Peter Mooney
Alfonso Monreal
Amanda Montgomery
Stephen Montgomery
Damien Morris
David Morris
Deirdre O'Connell
Eleanor O'Donovan
Tony Ó Gribín
Noreen O'Hare
Jack Pakenham
Mark Pepper
Robert Peters
Ann Quayle
Simon Reilly
Nicola Russell
Bridget Ryan
Dermot Seymour
Alison Shaw
Derek Smith
Nick Stewart
Elaine Thompson
Hilary Tully
Martin Wedge
Gordon Wilkinson
Chris Wilson
Sally Young

Anthony Bartley
Birth of the Kids. 1994. Acrylic and oil on canvas, 73 x 110 cms.

Una Bryce
Gravity. 1993. Oil on canvas, 180 x 240 cms.

Vivien Burnside
Produce. 1994. Tea chests, paint, chalk, 120 x 400 cms approx.

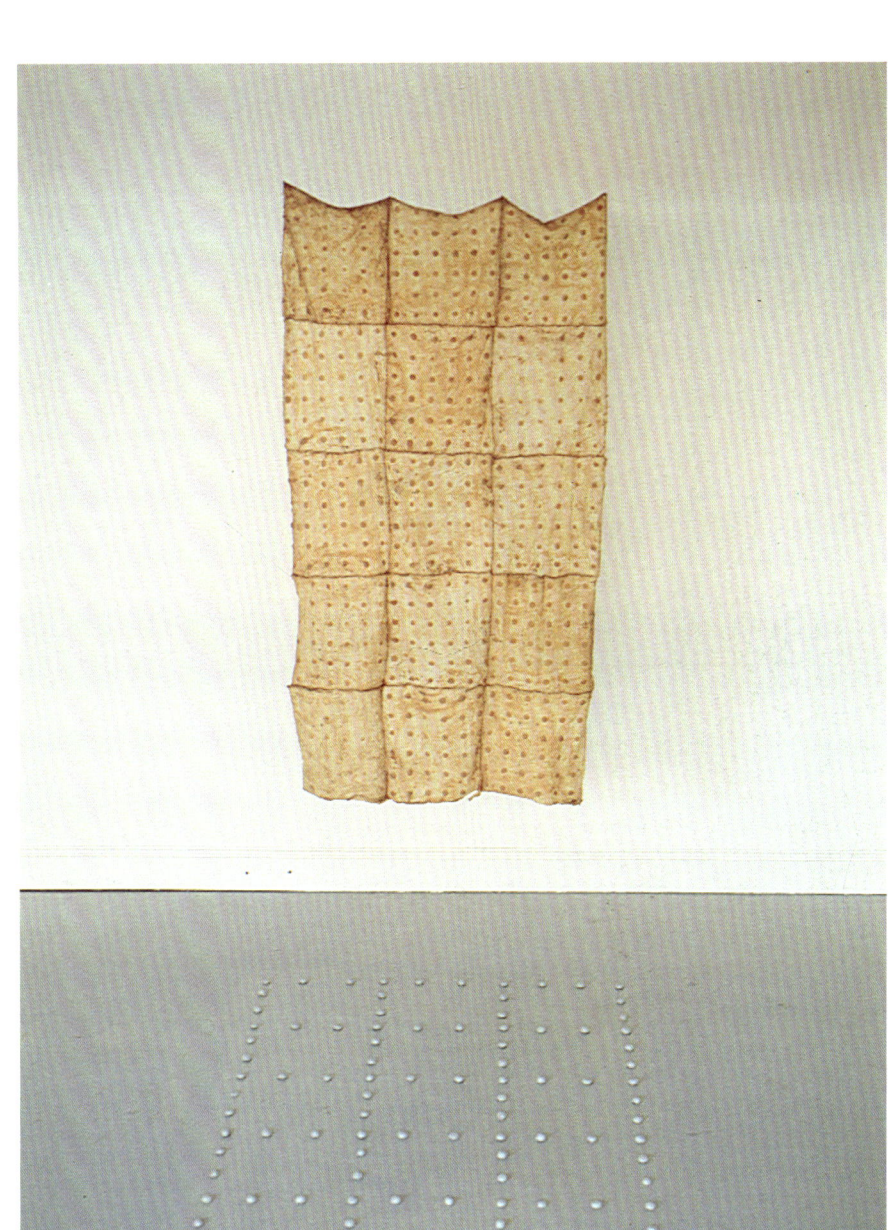

Lorraine Burrell
Braille. 1992. Latex and bolts, 213 x 91 cms.

Elaine Callen
Island of Moss. 1993. Pastel on paper, 64 x 49 cms.

Anne Clarke
Bricks. 1994. Acrylic and pastel on paper, 30 x 25 cms.

Brian Connolly
Seeing Device. 1993. Mixed media installation.

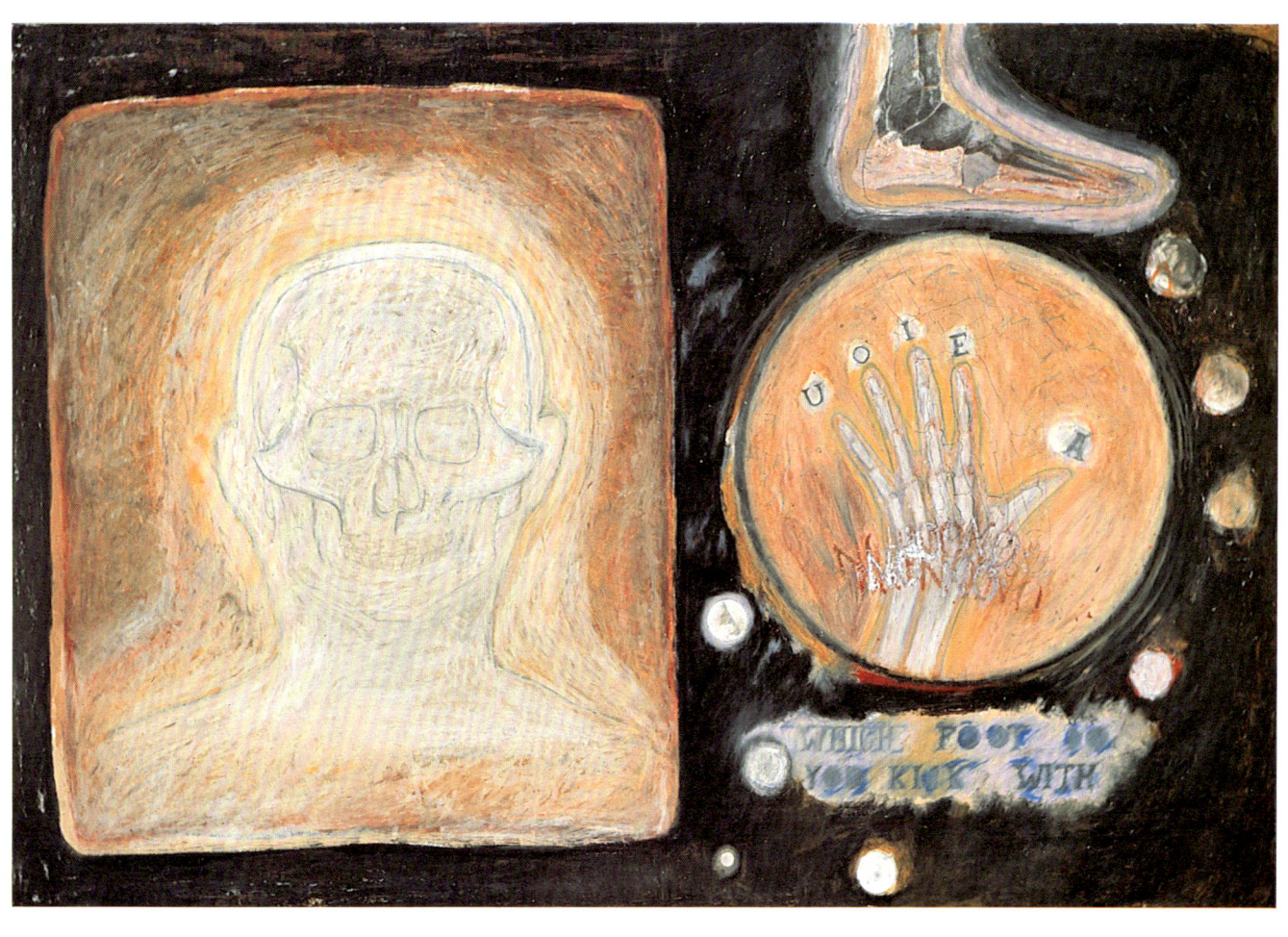

Damien Coyle
I Don't Remember. 1994. Pastel on paper, 70 x 100 cms.

Marie Thérèse Davis
Renaissance Man 2. 1994. Inks, chalk pastels, acrylics on canvas, 122 x 61 cms.

Gerry Devlin
Relics 1. Oil on canvas. 1993. 168 x 122 cms.

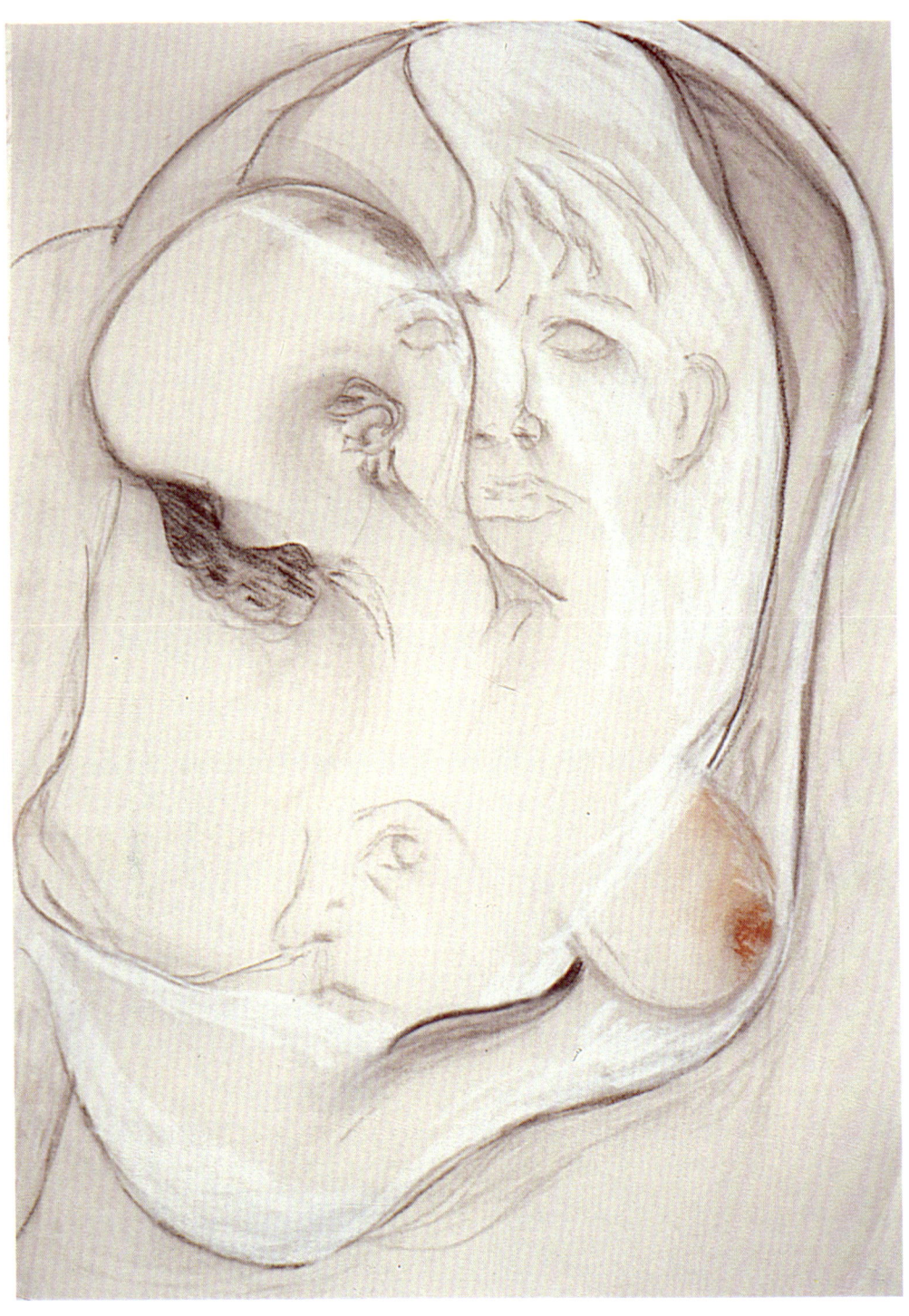

Moira Doherty
Master Race, Series 1.

Micky Donnelly
Meditation on Silence and Memory. 1993. Mixed media on canvas, 188 x 188 cms.

Frank Eyre
Rain on Window. 1993. Oil on canvas, 92 x 61 cms.

James Fearon
Portrait of Ken. 1992. Oil on canvas, 152 x 183 cms.

Paul Finnegan
Under the Moon. 1990. Mixed media on paper, 137 x 112 cms.

George Fleming
Time Moves On. 1990. Oil on canvas, 122 x 183 cms.

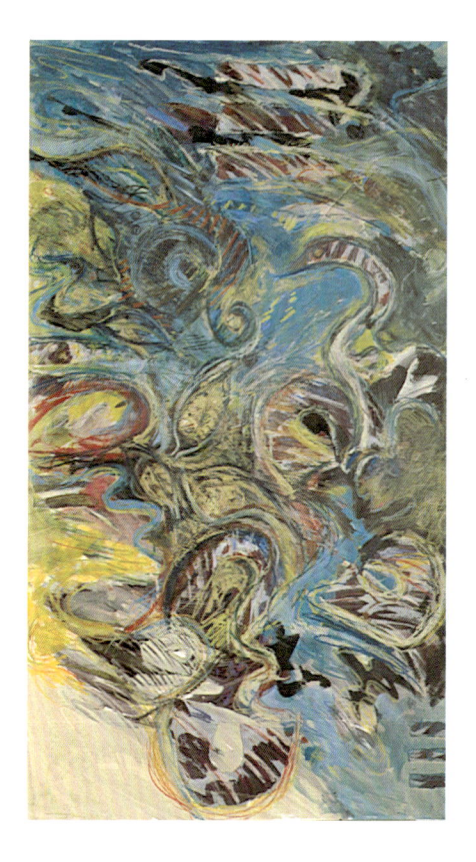

Nora Gaston
Ebb and Flow. 1993. Acrylic on paper (triptych). 130 x 210 cms.

Gerry Gleason
Ghost Dancer. 1993. Oil on canvas, 72 x 96 cms.

Nuala Gregory
Facture Series III. 1993. Monoprint on paper, 84 x 114 cms.

Ian Hamilton
An Cnoc. 1993. Oil on canvas, 61 x 51 cms.

John Hamilton
Untitled. 1990. Pastel on paper, 48 x 69 cms.

Kathy Herbert
Container. 1990. Peat, granite sand, heather, 420 x 120 cms.

Frank Holmes
The Wall. 1994. Acrylic on canvas, 72 x 92 cms.

Ronnie Hughes
Lessons in Perspective 3. 1993. Oil, wax on board, 41 x 41 cms.

Tim Johnson
Holopus Pepper Smile. 1993. Acrylic on paper.

Barbara Lavery
Six Shelved Vessels. 1993. Mixed media, 15 cms diameter.

Colette Lee
Unit System. 1993. Mixed media on canvas, 106 x 76 cms.

Terry McAllister
Coast. 1994. Oil on canvas (triptych), 181 x 110 cms.

Colin McGookin
The Sky High Cross. 1993.
Acrylic on wood and plastic, 61 x 248 cms.

Jim McKevitt
Car. 1993. Mixed media, 38 x 86 x 27 cms.

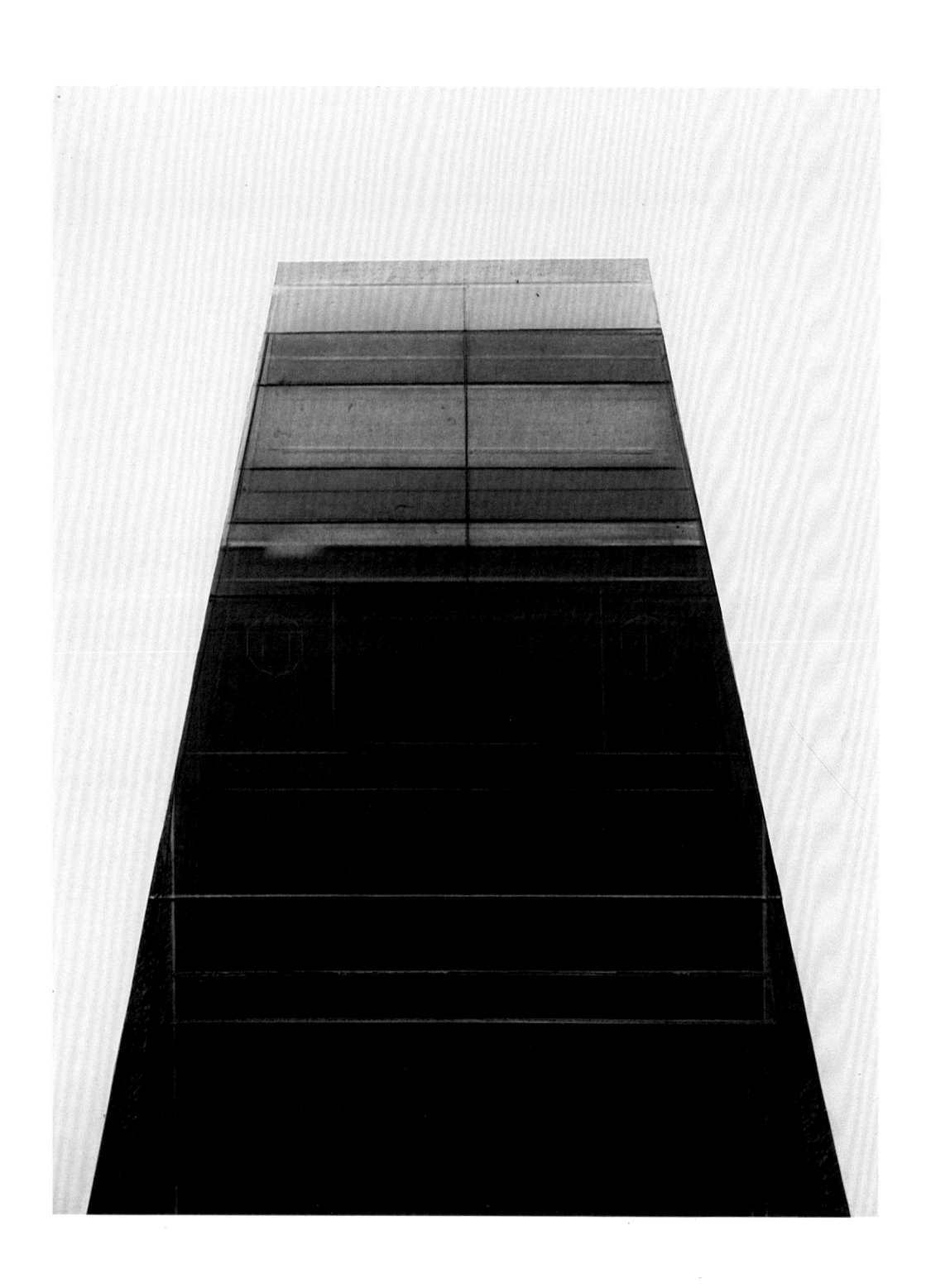

John Mathers
Armoured Vehicle, Image no. 1. 1994. Compressed charcoal on paper, 137 x 102 cms.

Michael Minnis
Cut Through No. 1. 1993. Acrylic on aluminium, 150 x 150 cms.

Alfonso López Monreal
Juana. 1993. Oil on canvas, 120 x 180 cms.

Amanda Montgomery
Inward Watching. 1991. Installation. Cement Fondue and Bark chips, 300 x 100 x 100 cms.

Deirdre O'Connell
Drawing from the Pompeianna series. 1992. Oil bar and pastel on paper, 41.5 x 30.5 cms.

Eleanor O'Donovan
Hybrid. 1993. Mixed media, 122 x 197 cms.

Tony Ó Gribín
Birth of an Irish Venus. 1993. Oil on linen, 221 x 141 cms.

Jack Pakenham
Le Dejeuner sur l'Herbe, (Ulster Version). 1993. Acrylic on board, 90 x 120 cms.

Mark Pepper
Deja Vu 1. 1992. Oil on canvas, 183 x 198 cms.

Robert Peters
Untitled. 1992. Chalk, 61 x 91 cms.

Simon Reilly
A Monument to a Great White Elephant. 1990. Oil on canvas, 205 x 155 cms.

Nicola Russell
Rosed Linen with Speculums. 1993. Oil on canvas, 152 x 203 cms.

Dermot Seymour
Perhaps the Bull From the North West has Already Come to the Conclusion of the Option to Float. 1993. Oil on canvas, 158 x 120 cms.

Derek Smith
Strata. 1990. Soil, sand and straw, 100 x 50 x 50cms.

Nick Stewart
Beyond the Pale. 1993. Site Specific Video Installation.

Elaine Thompson
Dormant. 1993. Suede, rubber tubing, glass, 200 x 10 x 10 cms.

Hilary Tully
Cosmic Source. 1993. Mixed media, 137 x 91 cms.

Martin Wedge
Untitled. 1993. Oil on canvas, 176 x 120 cms.

Chris Wilson
Returning Ground. 1989. Mixed media, 89 x 122 cms.

Sally Young
Mary, Mary Quite Contrary. 1993. Mixed media, 117 x 80 cms.

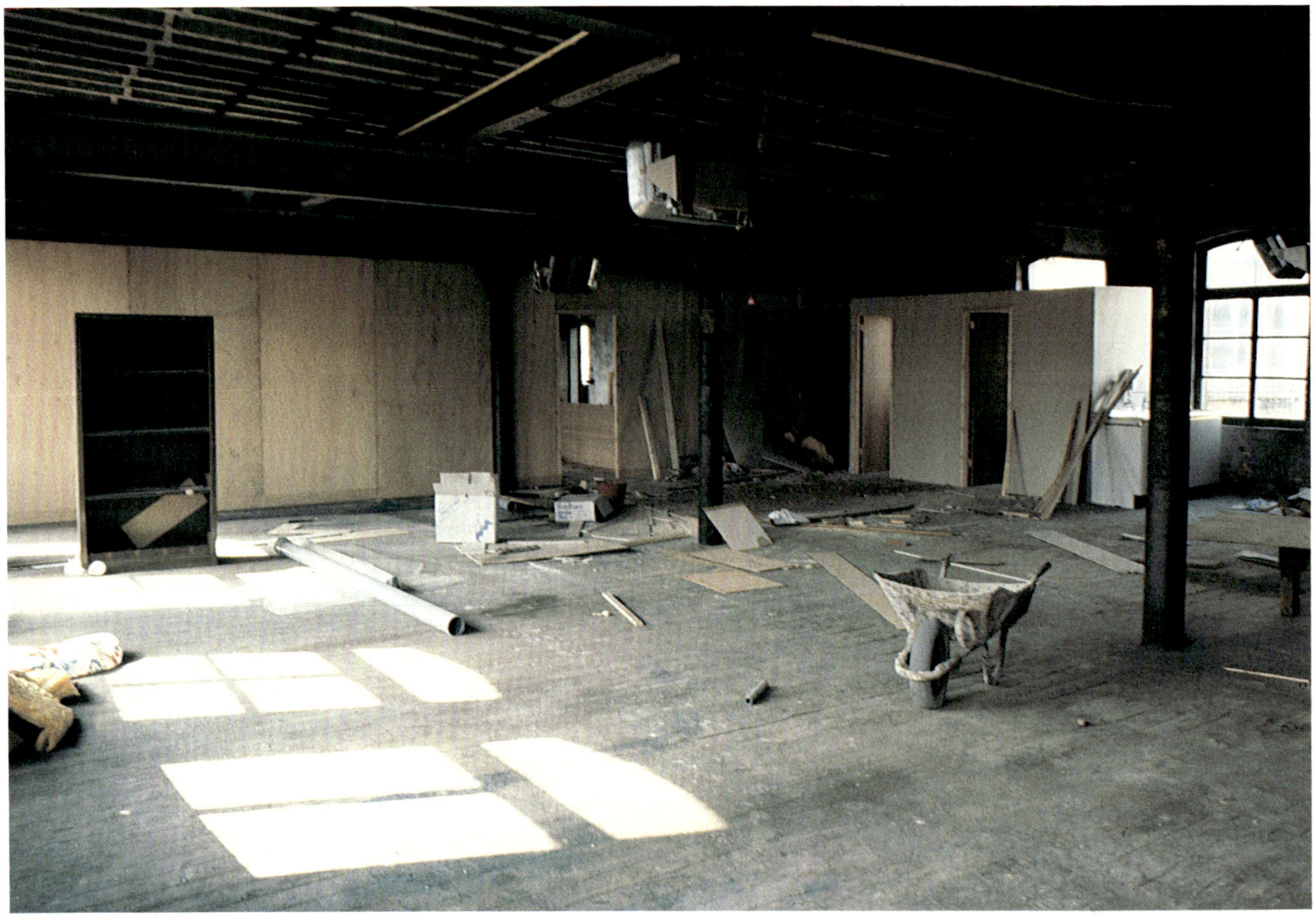

Reasons to be Artful ...?
Some issues for the artists of Queen Street Studios.

Herbert Marcuse used to tell the story of how during the Paris Commune of 1871, before they started shooting at people, the Communards shot at all the clocks in Paris and destroyed them. They did this because they were putting an end to the time of the Others, the time of their rulers, in order to reinvent a time of their own.[1]

On the Thursday 3 February 1994 edition of BBC Northern Ireland's Spotlight programme, Gerry Adams was shown 'speaking to the American people' in a dubbed American accent. Later in the same programme, he 'spoke' to us in a halting Belfast accent, not his own. The synchronisation of speech to lip movement, lip-sync, was the more accurate in the American case where the chances of its passing as true representation were never in question. The lip-sync mismatch in the second instance was expressly designed to achieve a similar effect of 'untruth' - the palpable implausibility of that disjunction between image and voice. The true voice proffered in each case was that of the narrator whose commentary organised and 'explained' the images making up the report.[2]

Whereas the Communards attempted a symbolic revolutionary and utopian gesture, BBC Northern Ireland was constrained by a political decree to so break the medium's rules of representation as to invite ridicule. The two stories have nothing in common other than to illustrate, when conveniently juxtaposed, that the political culture of Northern Ireland cannot sustain utopian aspirations; no 'solution' is even conceivable which could result in a new time, a clean break with oppressions of the past. At best we are fated to negotiate, accommodate and on occasions to obfuscate in order to contrive a settlement. The Spotlight programme illustrated one ordinary feature of this struggle, that 'truth' is not so much a casualty as a tendentious, if transparent, construction. We may yet have to converge upon such a 'truth' in order to survive.[3]

Northern Irish culture, as an arena of struggle, might be thought to be rich in representations of our various 'truths', political, historical and other. Is it not a commonplace that troubled situations bring forth great art? And does not great art contain 'truth'?

This essay will be concerned with an examination of these and related questions not so much in an attempt to answer them as to see whether and how they bear upon the work of one group of Belfast artists. A group whose sole relation is that each has occupied, at one time or another, a space in the Queen Street Studios complex. In the course of the argument, I hope to return to some of the comments made above.

In order to approach these questions, I shall begin with an (all too summary) account of what I take to be some of the key moments in the history of the relationship between art and philosophy. In so doing, I hope to arrive at some understanding of the limits of art: what it is that is expected of art and what art can and cannot legitimately say to us.

We begin (almost) at the beginning, with the story of ...
How Plato vanquished Homer and expelled the poets from the Republic.

This is the story of the 'ancient quarrel between philosophy and poetry' over which was to be the authentic bearer of truth. A putatively epistemological dispute, it was equally a struggle for intellectual leadership at a time of great upheaval in Athens, a period of dissent and revolution following military defeat. Up to the time of Socrates, epic poetry such as Homer's had formed the dominant mode of thinking of the age. It not only embodied the hero ethic sacred to Athenian culture but was revered as a repository of wisdom on all subjects, theoretical and practical. This poetic form of mythical thinking offered an organised understanding of human nature and the human world and a coherent vision of reality. The new practice of (Platonic) philosophy began, in part, by aggressively defining itself in opposition to such poetry as *the* source of superior wisdom. Plato borrowed the strategies of the Rhetoricians (another enemy) to demean art, defining it in negative terms as imitation or *mimesis*. Mimesis was a third order representation of truth, removed firstly from reality, which it imitated, and ultimately from the eternal Ideas which gave rise to the forms of reality. At a stroke, art was demoted to the third rate. Ironically, in accomplishing this, Plato's philosophy relied on elements of an existing epistemological and metaphysical orientation - borrowed from art itself. The ideal of knowledge as detached contemplation rather than inspired action reflects the attitude of the spectator at a drama or the viewer of fine art rather than the interventions of the epic hero; the idea that reality ultimately consists of harmoniously ordered forms whose contemplation affords sublime pleasure again suggests appreciation of the fine arts. Yet these ideas were to become the basis of a philosophy so ultimately hostile to art's claim on truth that Plato banished the poets from his ideal Republic as a corrupting element whose emphasis on merely sensuous beauty was an appeal to the lowest part of the soul. Philosophy, in contrast, developed the method of dialectical enquiry which when applied to aesthetic questions led to access to the transcendental Form of Beauty itself. In this, philosophy triumphed over art even within art's terrain.[4]

We can trace some of the forms of this triumphant philosophy in a schema proposed by Aristotle and modified (some 2,300 years later) by M.H. Abrams in his famous study 'The Mirror and The Lamp'. Aristotle set out to classify the various areas of knowledge according to subject matter, and to establish this knowledge upon sure foundations. He continued the Platonic attitude of treating art as a distinct realm of *fabricated objects* apart from ordinary life, and went on to define art as *poiesis* (making) in contrast to *praxis* (action). This effectively disenfranchised art in relation to the domains of action such as politics and ethics, just as Plato had relegated art to the realm of imitation rather than knowledge of reality. In order to explain, for example, a statue, Aristotle referred to its four 'causes': the material cause (the statue is made of bronze); the efficient cause (the statue was made by a sculptor); the formal cause (it is intended to resemble Pericles); the final cause (it was designed to commemorate and glorify the great statesman). This explained what the statue essentially was and how it came to be; the explanation itself constituted objective, scientific knowledge.

Abrams, in his first chapter, draws upon Aristotle's causes to provide a simple, diagrammatic scheme for discriminating various kinds of critical theory and practice. His four co-ordinates of art criticism are represented below:

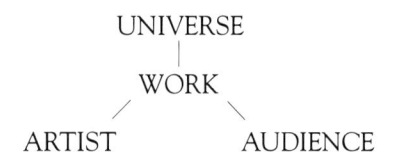

```
           UNIVERSE
              |
            WORK
           /    \
      ARTIST   AUDIENCE
```

Although any adequate theory must take account of all four elements, according to Abrams most theories tend to emphasise one element over the others. Thus we might say that a reading of a work which emphasises the work itself in isolation, as an autonomous whole, offers a 'formal' explanation ('objective' is Abrams preferred term). A theory which emphasises the creative power of the artist, the thoughts and feelings which went into the production of the work, is an expressive theory. Similarly for 'mimetic' theories (the work represents - imitates - some aspect of the world) and 'pragmatic' theories (the artist is primarily concerned with the effect of his or her work upon an audience).[5]

We might already begin to separate the Queen Street artists and their work into camps, each being construed as a more or less pure example of one or another of these approaches to art production (and consumption). And this might be fair: Queen Street Studios has produced no 'school', written no manifestos nor promoted any ideology. The sixty eight artists who have passed through the studios have worked as individuals, each pursuing his or her particular vision, practice or technique. Yet in jumping from Aristotle to Abrams, however plausibly, we have missed perhaps the key moment which determined the fate of modern art - the work of Immanuel Kant.

For Kant, as for all Enlightenment philosophers and reformers, the key to human nature was its inherent rationality, the inborn faculty of Reason. Yet, a devout Lutheran, he feared that science had begun to arrogate and specialise the uses of reason, relegating religion, politics and art to the realms of superstition, habit and sentiment. He self-consciously defined his mission as the need to "limit knowledge, in order to make room for faith".

Between 1781 and 1790, Kant produced three Critiques which together redefined what it meant to be a rational human being. In the Critique of Pure Reason, he restricted scientific judgement to the world of experiencable phenomena, describing how conceptual knowledge results from the mind's actively and necessarily imposing its forms upon nature. This greatly enriched the sense of the self (beyond the Cartesian 'locus and arbiter of knowledge') to become one source of our experience and, as such, a condition for the existence of our world. In the subsequent works, art and religion were re-established as matters of reason, open to argument and rational justification, but in the process each was assigned its particular (delimited) form of rationality, a language and practices appropriate only to itself. The world of knowledge and its conceptual mechanisms (Pure Reason) was held distinct from, and could in no wise legislate for, the realm of morality and politics (Practical Reason), while art was categorised with the ultimate questions about life and the universe which belonged to a separate order of Judgement.

Kant's legacy has been variously interpreted. To most philosophers, his is the greatest contribution since the Greeks. But for certain aestheticians and social scientists his influence, precisely because it has been so enormous and so inescapable, has contributed to 'problematic' developments within our culture.

The problem consists in that in categorically separating aesthetics from scientific truth and from universal morality, Kant paved the way for an autonomous art which could make no claims on truth nor on right action and so degenerated into 'mere art', art as object of fashion and matter of taste. For Weber and Habermas, this separation is constitutive of a Modernity in which modern art has been "expelled" from modern societies - i.e. expelled from the "constitutive, cognitive and practical mechanisms producing and reproducing societal modernity".[6] In other words, art has lost its capacity to speak the truth concerning our most fundamental engagements and commitments. J.M. Bernstein calls this loss 'aesthetic alienation'. The challenge, as he sees it, is to reconnect art and truth - to experience art as somehow cognitive (truth bearing) and truth as somehow sensuous and particular. Others see it as the need to connect art and life, to broaden the aesthetic to include the everyday.[7]

Bernstein applies his diagnosis to the philosophy of art rather than to art practice, but there is evidence enough of Kant's legacy within the arts themselves. The 19th Century *L'art pour l'art* movement is the clearest possible realisation of Kant's theory of an art freed from the influence of history, politics and every social concern. In the post-war period we have had Ad Reinhardt's *art as art* followed by Joseph Kosuth's extreme variation on autonomous art.[8] Other candidates from the 70s and 80s might be Neo-Geo and 'hands off' art.[9] Meanwhile, back in the realm of criticism, Clement Greenberg was almost programmatically extending Kant's critique to the practice of painting.[10]

Greenberg ascribes a Kantian logic to the Modernist movement in its recognition of the need to limit painting to its unique area of competence in order to preserve it - and the other arts - from assimilation to "entertainment pure and simple" and thenceforth to therapy. Greenberg's 1961 essay 'Modernist Painting' has "come to typify the Modernist critical position on the visual arts"; his influence on American painting has been enormous. Greenberg, theorising Modernist logic, determined that painting had to divest itself of everything that it might share with sculpture; so out went modelling, shading, figuration and every suggestion of or association with three dimensional space. The result was a flatness and abstraction so uncompromising that it almost certainly contributed to the great turn away from painting which followed the reign of the Abstractionisms - the turn to photography and language, to installation, and to the recontextualisation of the artwork. This begs the question: is it the case that each new medium or genre is merely granted a period of maturation before it too is called to account at the court of Kantian logic and immanent critique - have we reached the point at which only a pluralist and arational Postmodernism can save them? Or can all the art practices be retheorised along lines suggested by Bernstein, or Dewey, or Adorno?[11]

These unhappy questions need to be grounded somehow. I shall attempt to relate them to the context of the Queen Street Studios, to the political situation which informs and deforms these artists' work. But first, yet another detour - through Kant's notion of Taste and Bernstein's bold claim that the (post-Kantian) discourse of aesthetics is proto-political and marks the absence of a truly political domain in modern societies. I shall then offer some observations on the condition of aesthetic and political discourse in Northern Ireland.

In his Critique of Judgement, Kant examined the kind of judgement we make when we feel and state that something is beautiful - what he called the Judgement of Taste. The defining characteristics of such a Judgement are that it is (1) contemplative and disinterested; (2) it has the feeling of knowledge but does not involve conceptual knowledge; (3) it is objective in that it may legitimately demand universal agreement; (4) it is a free judgement - free from desire, from the demands of morality, and from any definite concept of beauty; (5) it involves recognition that works of art are ends in themselves - they have 'purposiveness without purpose'. This has developed into the view that "to experience something aesthetically is to experience the perceived properties of the object and to do so *for the sake of the perception rather than for the sake of any other relation in which one may stand to the object*".[12] This accords with Greenberg's dictum that the arts had to demonstrate that the kind of experience they provided was valuable in its own right and not to be obtained elsewhere.

We can recognise in all of this the still dominant notion that cultivation of taste is necessary to the understanding of art and that art can only be meaningfully discussed in terms of Taste. Taste differs from science in that it requires no concepts by which to judge; from morality and politics in that it is free from interest - interest in the condition of the world. Is it so surprising that Bernstein asks:

> "What can we make of a domain in which questions of truth, goodness, efficacy, even pleasure (since our interest in art is 'disinterested') are eliminated at the outset? What sort of beast might beauty be if in considering it we are not considering how the world is (truth), how we do or should comport ourselves in the world (morality), or what might be useful or pleasurable to us?"

Art has been expelled from ordinary life and forced to seek alternative accommodation. Having been lured everywhere, and still homeless, it has taken refuge in the marketplace. Consider its fate: Art has been (con)fused with aesthetics and restricted to the fine arts, or expanded to subsume Life itself; 'enjoyable but functionless' art has been defined in binary opposition to 'practical but disagreeable labour' - the one gratuitous, the other forced and mercenary; art has served as badge and requisite of the elite or become the entire community's prerogative; art has been pressed into service for ideological and political ends[13] or abandoned as subjective and powerless.

If Kant tried to establish the ground rules for any legitimate discourse about art - to confine our remarks to edifying notions of Beauty, Form, Taste, Genius, The Sublime etc. - the struggle since has been to apply, modify or disrupt these rules. We can continue to speak a rarefied language of aesthetics or attempt to reconnect art to all that it has been sundered from and forbidden to speak of. Rather than enquire into the current conditions of possibility of legitimate aesthetic statements, we can turn our attention to what artists are actually doing. It then becomes a question of how artists deal with the burden of influence and turn it to account. And this marks a movement from a discourse of aesthetics to a discourse of art practice.

Aesthetics (in its late 18th Century coinage) referred to subjective sense activity, meaning: the perception of material things through the senses, as distinct from the apprehension of immaterial objects in thought. The term was only gradually associated with art and restricted to objects whose express purpose was to exist *as* aesthetic (now defined as artistic or beautiful) artefacts.[14] Discourse on aesthetics became increasingly abstract and technical, with a marked imbrication of ideas on the autonomy and self-determination of the aesthetic artefact with that of the bourgeois subject. In the process, the discourse itself took on a quasi-ideological form and function[15] which compromised its objects while securing their value to society. It is only in this century that artworks have been consistently created in opposition to a normative aesthetic, to the extent that it has become questionable whether philosophical aesthetics can or should keep pace with changing art practices, or give way to new or other forms of discourse more adequate to the task of bringing understanding to art, or art to understanding.[16]

In advancing his claim that aesthetics today is a proto-political domain and that art, as practice, mounts a challenge to theory, Bernstein refers to the current state of scientific and cultural theory. Post-positivism, he tells us, has undermined the isolation of scientific 'truth' from normative and aesthetic values and contributed to a debate in which artworks must be understood in non-aesthetic terms. Within science itself, one might add, it is communities of scientists whose shared cultural values help determine what counts as science, and aesthetic considerations influence the construction of models (and concomitant theses) as well as the success of 'elegant' over 'convoluted' theories. It would appear that the Kantian divisions are being challenged also from within the autonomous disciplines.

Bernstein goes on to provide an analysis of just how art departs from the dominance of theory: art authorises unique, individual works which refuse the hierarchy of universal over particular; as sensuous particulars these works celebrate embodiment as opposed to concept; and finally, artistic practices in the realm of sensuousness and embodiment instigate a new conception of acting - a combination of doing and making, of *praxis* and *poiesis*. Bernstein claims that this threefold departure opens the possibility of a knowing and truth outside of theoretical knowing and truth.[17]

Post-aesthetic theories (*pace* Kant) correspondingly locate the meaning of art in its cognitive dimension. This is not so strange if we remember, for example, that icon and religious painting had a largely cognitive function at a time of widespread illiteracy. And that history painting, with its narratives and codes, long dominated traditional art in the West. We might also bear in mind that truth, although philosophically a property of language, was defined by Nietzsche as a 'mobile army of metaphors'. If art can help us understand and engage with the world, create new and useful metaphors for feelings and conditions, there can be no denying its 'truth value'.

But we are running ahead of the proto-political argument, which is founded on a historical analysis ranging from Plato to the moment of Modernity. It may be summarised as follows. In its suppression by philosophy, art was consigned to the world of opinion (*doxa*) as opposed to theory, and to the world of appearance as opposed to essence or reality. But opinion and appearance are the very worlds of politics once politics ceases to be understood as applied theory. Art and politics were suppressed by Plato in a double moment of domination which served the interests of a narrow rationality. It was not until Kant's theory of Taste that there was a return to "the consideration of appearances in their own right together with concepts of communication, intersubjective agreement, and shared judgement that are constitutive for emphatic, autonomous political thinking". This indicates a movement away from theory towards a free evaluation, through common sense (*sensus communis*), of particulars as they appear to us. If we agree to act on this evaluation, we have shifted from the realm of aesthetics to that of everyday politics. Thus Hannah Arendt looked to Kant's aesthetics for Kant's politics, and Bernstein, more boldly, affirms that: "Speculatively, art and politics are one. Beauty bereaved is politics bereaved" (p13). And (p269) " ... we can best understand the inability of modernity to unfold, its resistance to real [political] transformation, through the separation of art and politics".

For Bernstein, art's autonomous vocation is unstable and unsustainable. He insists that we interrogate art historically to see what it has been and what it has become. Building upon this, he believes, theorists might uncover conceptual resources for the transformation of the world. Terry Eagleton, for example, raises the possibility of an emancipatory sense of the aesthetic as part of a knowledge which "locates the unity of fact and value in the practical, critical activity of men and women - in a form of understanding which is brought to birth in the first place by emancipatory interests, which is bred and deepened in active struggle, and which is an indispensible part of the realisation of value".[18] Meanwhile, the artist too might consider renewed possibilities. Which of the elements of Abrams diagram should s/he privilege: the expressive, the pragmatic, the formal? Or are new relationships and forms necessary to a combined *praxis / poiesis* which would cast off the yoke of received aesthetic ideas?

More questions. Still, the answers will not come from within theory but from such new practices as may emerge from renewed understanding. Whether we see them emerge in Northern Ireland is perhaps the pressing question.

There is much that militates against such a possibility. In our adversarial political culture, the artist is called upon to recognise or discountenance politics - and in either case is mocked. To embrace politics is to exploit them, to refuse them is to evade our primary reality. But can the artist be so easily arraigned? In Northern Ireland we lack either a vigorous political culture of citizen participation which might more fully incorporate art practices, or the revolutionary potential which mobilises populations and may incidentally throw up new art forms, practices or movements. The Left/Right struggle of social democracy has been replaced by a fundamentally sectarian one. Instead of difference and pluralism, we have division and antagonism; all history is applied history is politics; and politics is played as a factional zero-sum game in which winner takes all. Since there is neither credible politics nor utopian hope, such political artwork as is produced tends to eschew advocacy for a psychological or social commentary which is often layered and oblique. For the very good reasons that overt political advocacy is (1) institutionally discouraged and (2) dangerous - to the artist and to the institution which displays the work. Whatever the constitution of 'properly political' art, I do not know of a single artist in Belfast who propagandises through art, whose work represents a party political ideology.[19]

And this in spite of the already large, and growing, number of practising artists in Belfast. This growth is a phenomenon in need of study but it is such as to already give rise to speculation that, in Belfast at least, the visual arts may come to prominence, eclipsing the traditional Irish strengths in literature and drama. Why this might be so cannot be addressed in such a short essay. I shall approach the question from a 'psychological' point of view only, through some brief remarks on notions of creativity and identity as mediated through local conditions.[20]

Charles Taylor, in his work on the philosophy of the subject, has suggested a close analogy between self-discovery and artistic creation:

> "With Herder, and the expressivist understanding of human life, the relation becomes very intimate. Artistic creation becomes the paradigm mode in which people can come to self-definition. The artist becomes in some way the paradigm case of the human being, as agent of original self-definition. Since about 1800, there has been a tendency to heroize the artist, to see in his or her life the essence of the human condition, and to venerate him or her as a seer, the creator of cultural values.
>
> But of course, along with this has gone a new understanding of art. No longer defined mainly by imitation, by mimesis of reality, art is understood now more in terms of creation. The two ideas go together. ... I discover myself through my work as an artist, through what I create ... and through this and this alone I become what I have it in me to be. Self-discovery requires *poiesis*, making." [21]

In the current context, the emphasis on *poiesis* immediately invites contrast with *praxis*, and indeed Taylor goes on to recount how self-definition was soon contrasted with morality and, by extension, politics. The practices of making and doing are maintained in a steady separation throughout the Romantic period, as they partake in the shifting combinations of concepts which come to define the modern idea of the Self. At this point, the notion of authenticity is introduced and comes to be defined in parallel to that of the aesthetic. Each is categorised as autotelic, an end in itself. Whereas the aesthetic concerned a cultivation of particular feelings, authenticity had to do with the more general idea of attending to our 'inner voice' as the source of the true Self, as opposed to the demands of external forces such as social duty or an imperious God. Thus as the subject mutates it moves centre stage in a culture which is becoming increasingly anthropocentric. To the secular humanist imagination, self-definition and authenticity signified original modes of self-creation, involving a revolt against convention. In a similar vein, the role of the artist was no longer to mimic reality but to create: originally, freely, drawing inspiration from inner nature and flying in the face of prevailing artistic and social conditions. Often the three concepts (authenticity, self-definition, the aesthetic) came together - in the figures of the aesthete and the *flâneur*, and latterly in the postmodern 'aestheticisation of the self'. Morality, it must be noted, is throughout construed as a force of oppression, crushing instinct and desire (the inner life) and enforcing compliance with an abstract, heteronomous regime of order. Thus the demand for truth to self finally comes to be valued above that of intersubjective justice, leading to a 'self-determining freedom' which, for Taylor, is a problematic development. When the freedom to create one's own values also becomes an end in itself, it issues in modern forms of subjectivity which have taken an extreme turn away from recognition of existing structures of meaning and value, as well as from the need to forge the self through dialogue with different others.[22]

To apply all of this to our own situation in Northern Ireland, we need only raise the question of identity. Metaphysically speaking, identity is an attempt to elevate to idealist abstraction some concrete particular(s). It might be thought that in the constitution of a socio-political identity, the aesthetic (and the ideological) would have a role to play: confirming individuals in the belief that their inner nature is in harmony with the social order, while supplying a reassuring sense of wholeness of the self as one among a community of similarly constituted selves.

But, as we have noted, identity in Northern Ireland is predominantly a matter of enforced, binary opposition, a violent stabilising of what is ambiguous, precarious, and unformed. In a situation in which the Constitution itself is the primary issue, the interaction of ideas of the self and the identity of the nation becomes more than an analogy - it becomes a mortal matter. Our identities are narrowly determined and virulently reinforced through concepts of religion and nationality in such a way as to overwhelm any attempt to alter the terms of definition. Radical, democratic forms of collective action do not exist and attempts by individuals to redescribe or redefine themselves through personal narrative or an aesthetics of the self are seen as patently illusory. Instead we have a widespread aestheticisation of politics, extraordinary to the visitor. The visual environment is awash with symbols of one or another political absolute, forever gesturing foreclosure on the subject.

Which perhaps helps explain why our local artists have never produced any recognisable form of that much sought after 'regional art'. Regional art requires a sense of place and belonging, but also of community and shared purposes. Here, community is fractured, purposes uncertain and divergent, and continual demand made on the individual to conform to pre-given national and religious identity. Also, in place of theory, we have rhetorical claims about Irish art - the twin fallacies of determinism and essentialism. Irish art is either (to be?) galvanised by the political turmoil or reflects the essential (national) characteristics of its producers: art by stereotype.

Nevertheless, the artist who would transcend all of this risks cultivating delusion. S/he is in a position similar to that of Kant's dove who thought that but for the resistance of the air around, s/he would be able to fly in total freedom. Which is not to say that art cannot embody a form of refusal of politics, or an enquiry into other than political effects. Or seek out a form of politics (feminism, eco-politics) other than our staple brand, one which might bring personal development and political action closer together. Richard Rorty has suggested that we can adopt an ironic outlook and aestheticise the self through a self-chosen vocabulary of private development which is quite separate from a public vocabulary of politics or social justice.[23] But Rorty insists that the two vocabularies cannot be reconciled at the level of theory. Can they be reconciled in a work of art or in a renewed art practice? Or, as Adorno suggests, is it the principle of art to seek out and synthesise such incompatible elements so as to confront the given reality with what it is not, but what it could well be?[24]

Broadly speaking, some of the older generation of artists in Queen Street Studios have attempted to address the political side of this relation, the younger artists seem more comfortable with work which is expressive of personal concerns or derives from developments within art itself. Of course, these are not the only possibilities, there are many ways and reasons for making art. Yet, in Northern Ireland, it cannot be said to be easy. Whatever residual status the profession of artist may have in modern Ireland, as creator of cultural values or harbinger of new identities, the artist's material conditions generally border on genteel (or not so genteel) poverty. And our state support systems can only be characterised as a case of benign neglect. That there are so many practising artists in Belfast might be taken as a sign of hope, of a series of personal attempts to break through stereotyped identity, to present to the public new modes of making and doing. Or read as a resort to private pursuits as part of a refusal of a horrific public politics. The option for creativity, in time of recession, in a situation in which available forms of identity are felt to be untenable, is an aid to the beleagured self. But to make a career of it? Are the reasons to be artful so compelling? Marcuse has suggested that they are,[25] but we must ask the artists, or, better still, look to their work for an answer.

(An open) Conclusion

This essay has been largely a story of oppressions and denials. Historically, of the oppression of art by philosophy and the denial of art's claim to truth. And locally, of the denial of art's contribution to society - to the redefinition of identities and forms of engagement with the world - through the lack of support structures, of opportunities to work, to experiment and to exhibit. I recognise a didactic strain in the essay and must confess that, in the course of the writing, it mutated from being a reflection on issues in the artwork to becoming an address to the artists. The strain may well show, but I feel that the lack of informed debate among artists has been a major problem hampering the development of the visual arts in Northern Ireland.

The artists of Queen Street Studios, through the production of this catalogue, but so much more so through their continued existence as a flagship studio group, have demonstrated the will to enter into and open out that debate. A debate which will enquire into the political as well as the aesthetic, and do so through works of art as much as through discourse. A debate which hopefully will surprise us with emergent truths and lead to strong works of art with an authentic base in local conditions, works able to compete with the best of contemporary art without apeing or deferring to it.

If art is such enquiry, Adorno has suggested that it is also the future-oriented pursuit of truth. The statement is a promise as well as a challenge, one to which our local artists might respond. And what, in 1994, might they make of Lukacs assertion that the great artist is no disinterested observer but 'a partisan for the truth'?

Paddy Donnelly, 1994

1. 'Dialectics of Liberation', edited David Cooper, p202. Penguin Books 1968.

2. These are not the only questions of 'truth' arising from this situation - we are used to gauging the veracity of a person's testimony from the nuances of expression, composure of voice and other signals. A voice-over denies us these; the news is not giving us the truth ...?

3. These 'truths' are multiplying. Witness the phenomenon of revised and revisionist histories in Irish academia, cultural criticism and politics.

4. See Richard Schusterman, 'Pragmatist Aesthetics, Living Beauty, Rethinking Art', Chapter 2. Blackwell Publishers, Cambridge, Massachussets, 1992.

5. M.H. Abrams, 'The Mirror and the Lamp; romantic theory and the critical tradition', Oxford University Press, 1953. The mirror of the title refers to art (and philosophy) holding up a mirror to nature; the lamp is a reference to the mind casting its light upon the world. As the lamp metaphor came to displace that of the mirror, so Abrams periodises the successive forms of criticism. The mimetic dominated from Plato through the Roman era, the pragmatic from then to the late 18th Century, the expressive from Romanticism to the early 20th Century. It was only in his own time (the 1950s) that formalism ('the objective point of view') became the 'reigning mode' of criticism.

6. A second expulsion for art. See J.M. Bernstein, 'The Fate of Art, Aesthetic Alienation from Kant to Derrida and Adorno'. Polity Press, 1992.

7. See John Dewey, 'Art as Experience', 1934, reprinted 1987 by Southern Illinois University Press as volume 10 of 'The Late Works of John Dewey'. Dewey's pragmatist definition of art aims at "recovering the continuity of aesthetic experience with normal processes of living". He includes among the aesthetic such experiences as the tidying of a room or participation in sport.

8. Kosuth is an interesting case of mediated Kantian influences: his analogy between art and the analytic proposition, art as tautology, derives from a mix of Kantian ideas (as does much of modern philosophy); his desire to reinstate the conceptual element in works of art is anti-Kantian; yet his valorisation of the artist as creator (of new art propositions) is a version of Kant's notion of genius. See his influential essay 'Art after Philosophy', 1969, reprinted in Art in Theory 1900-1990, edited by Charles Harrison and Paul Wood, Blackwell 1992.

9. See 'New Art' edited Andreas Papadakis et al, Academy Editions, London 1991, p66, in which Robert Rosenblum uses the term 'hands off' in contrast to 'hand-made' to describe art which eschews traditional painterly or sculptural practice to reflect the world of commerce, signs, images, television etc. Such work has been described as an attempt to eliminate subjectivity and to go directly to the materials, or to the processes represented. Nevertheless, there is a pronounced strain of Kantian 'purposiveness without purpose' about it - the fact that it has the look of something potentially functional only serves to accentuate its functionlessness. The work I have in mind has commodity form, commodity production values and processes (the conceptual artist, the Master, delegates the labour to a

contractor i.e. apprentice or artisan) and possesses exchange value without use value - perhaps even as 'art'. It becomes an art freed from 'labour' as toil and time (praxis) using up life; it attempts to transcend mortality, to become - what? - the Pure Art Idea, the essential Form of the Commodity, or a postmodern appropriation of Renaissance relations of (art) production?

10. Clement Greenberg, 'Modernist Painting', 1961, reprinted in 'Art in Theory 1900-1990', edited by Charles Harrison and Paul Wood, Blackwell 1992.

11. For Adorno, all authentic art contains a utopian moment. It confronts and negates the given reality; it is "an illusion in which another reality shows forth". He saw art as one pole of opposition to an instrumental reason which reduces the identity of people and things to functions of something else. Hence his claim that "Insofar as one can speak of a social function of works of art, it lies in their functionlessness ... the useless alone represents what at one point might become useful, the happy use". And: "There is something contradictory to the idea of a conservative work of art". Quotes taken from 'The Essential Frankfurt Reader', edited Andrew Arato et al, Continuum Publishing Company, New York, 1982, pp 220-222.

12. Oswald Hanfling, 'Philosophical Aesthetics,' 1992, Open University Press, p144, italics mine.

13. Examples are Soviet Socialist Realism, and, on the American side, see 'Abstract Expressionism, Weapon of the Cold War' by Eva Cockroft reprinted in 'Art and Modern Culture' edited Francis Frascina et al, Phaidon Press 1992.

14. See Raymond Williams, 'Keywords', 1976, Fontana, for a history of the term.

15. See Terry Eagleton, 'The Ideology of The Aesthetic', Blackwell 1990. On *form*, see pp93-94: "The aesthetic, one might argue, is in this sense the very paradigm of the ideological ... Like aesthetic judgements for Kant, ideological utterances conceal an essentially emotive content within a referential form, characterising the lived relation of a speaker to the world in the act of appearing to characterise the world". On *function*, see pp22-25 where Eagleton describes how the aesthetic intervenes as a "dream of reconciliation" between a civil society composed of individuals with competing economic interests and a political state founded on abstract (universal) rights - to form a notional community deceptively, if consensually, constituted.

16. I refer to the hegemony of Anglo-American analytic aesthetics in its attempt to bring logical rigour to bear on art interpretation. This is being successfully challenged by Continental critical discourses which investigate art in its historical and contextual settings; and latterly by a form of paraliterature (half criticism, half literature) which seems to want to usurp the power and status of the artwork itself.

17. Bernstein does not prescribe new forms of truth nor propose new models of cognition. However, one possibility is the 'emancipatory knowledge' mentioned by Terry Eagleton in his 'The Ideology of The Aesthetic'. See further remarks below.

18. Terry Eagleton, 'The Ideology of The Aesthetic', Blackwell 1990.

19. For a synopsis of the debate over political art, see Jennifer Todd, 'Georg Lukacs, Walter Benjamin, and the Motivation to make Political Art' in Radical Philosophy #28, Summer 1981.

20. See Seamus Deane, 'Critical Reflections', Artforum, December 1993, for remarks on the uneven development of Irish art forms and the possibility of a fully historical explanation.

21. Charles Taylor, 'The Ethics of Authenticity', Harvard University Press 1991, pp61-62.

22. Ibidem. For Taylor, what this leads to is the phenomena of social atomisation, anomie, and a debilitated political culture of non-participation and inertia. His response is to call for, among other things, a vigorous politics of free initiatives, collective action and democratic will-formation - around issues and projects which are realistic and achievable while inherently advancing empowerment.

23. Richard Rorty, 'Contingency, Irony and Solidarity', Cambridge University Press, 1989

24. 'The Essential Frankfurt Reader', edited Andrew Arato et al, Continuum Publishing Company, New York, 1982

25. Herbert Marcuse interviewed in 'Dialogues with contemporary Continental thinkers', by Richard Kearney, Manchester University Press, 1984, states that:

> "Man must never cease to be an artist, to criticise and negate his present self and society and to project by means of his creative imagination alternative 'images of existence'. He can never cease to imagine because he can never cease to change".

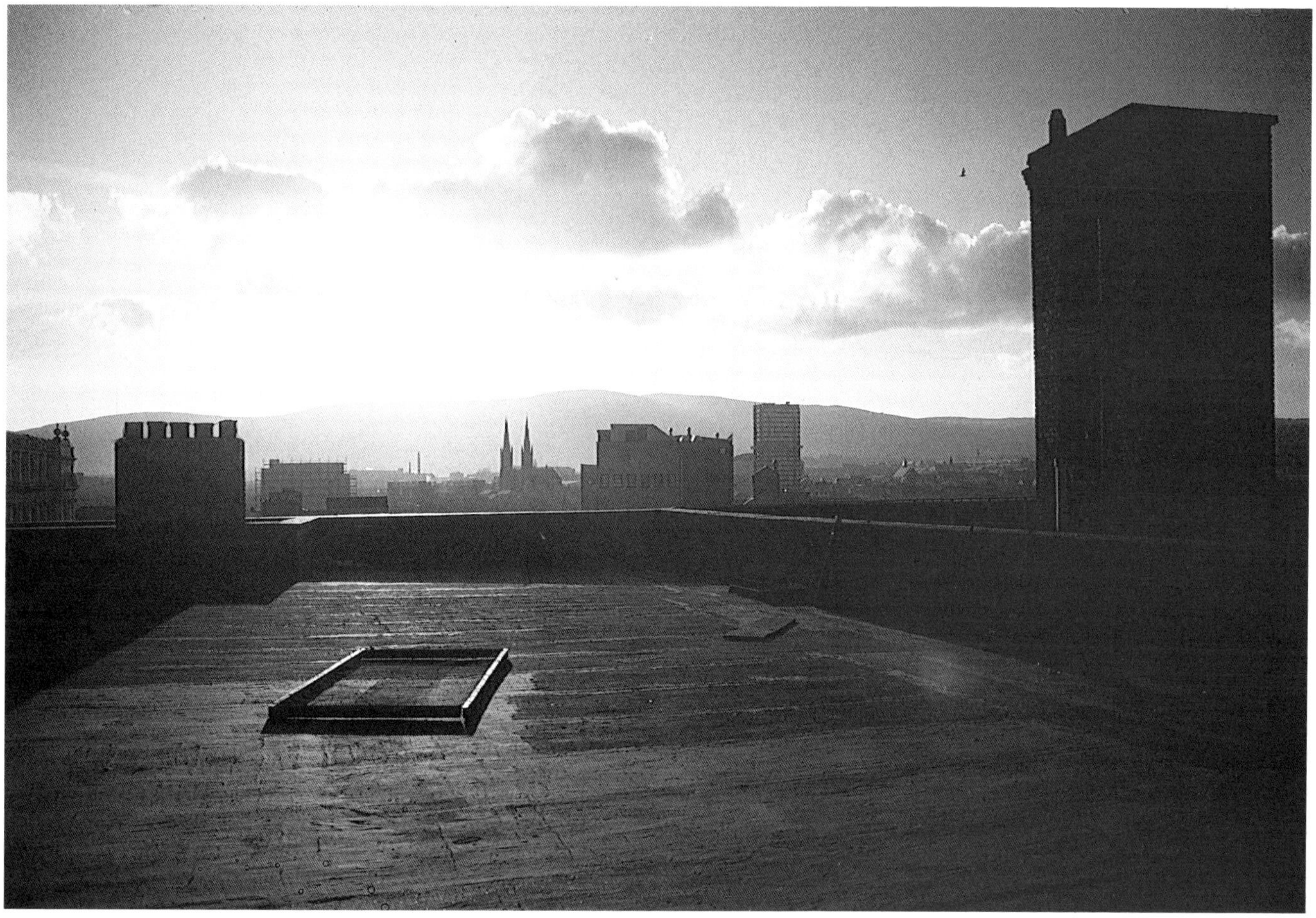

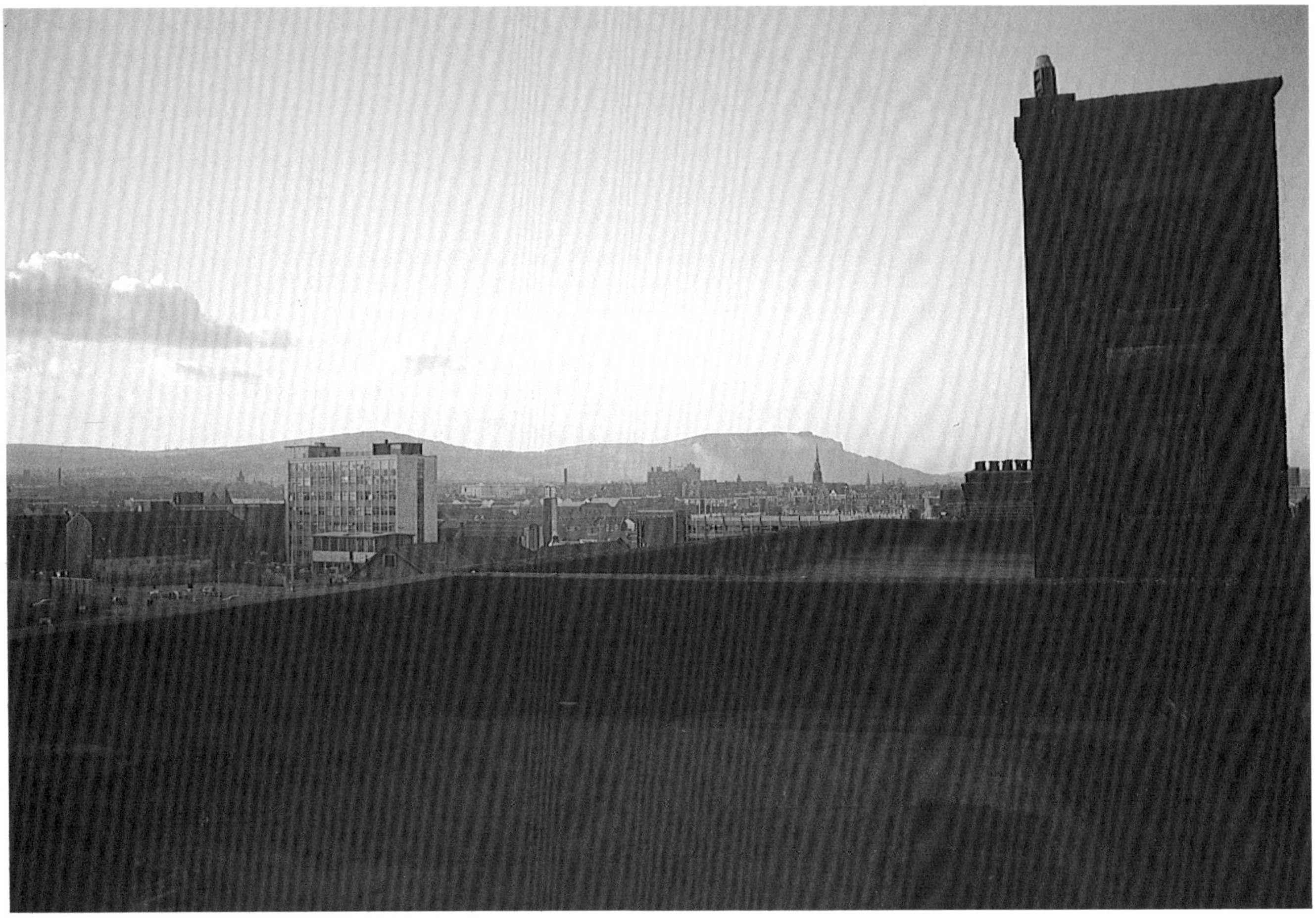

Anthony Bartley

Currently living in Belfast and a recent graduate of the University of Ulster at Belfast, (1985-1989), Bartley has exhibited, in the interim, in Ireland (Belfast, Sligo and Claremorris) and Holland. He has also participated in Slide Shows to live music and poetry readings and performance art (Antwerp 1992; Belfast 1993); as well as contributing to Circa and Fortnight magazines. Bartley is the Visual Arts Editor for Gown Literary Supplement. A part-time instructor with the National Schizophrenia Fellowship, Bartley has been active in the Art Therapy movement.

Una Bryce

Having completed her Foundation course in Liverpool and graduated from Coventry Polytechnic, Bryce went on to study in Birmingham Polytechnic, where she was awarded an MA in Fine Art Painting (1988). Since then she has exhibited extensively in Northern Ireland as well as in England and Greece. She has held a Fellowship at the Limerick College of Art and Design where she was Artist in Residence (1991-1992). Bryce has also worked in Education and was a visiting lecturer at the Cork and Limerick Colleges of Art.

Vivien Burnside

Having completed her BA in Fine Art at the University of Ulster, Burnside as a practicing artist, worked as an Arts Administrator and part time tutor for a number of years in Belfast before returning to study for her MA (1993-1995). She has had several one-person exhibitions (Riverside, Coleraine 1983; Grapevine, Dublin 1983; Crescent, Belfast 1984; and Blue Coat Gallery, Liverpool 1985); as well as participating in group exhibitions (among them, Women on Women, Fenderesky Gallery 1986; Irish Women Artists, Douglas Hyde Gallery 1987; Relocating History, Fenderesky Gallery at Queen's and Orchard Gallery, Derry 1993). In 1992, Burnside spent a period in Florence (Arts Council Bursary and Travel Award) where she studied Renaissance Drawing. Most recently she has been Artist in Residence at the Crescent Arts Centre, Belfast.

Lorraine Burrell

Since her graduation from Liverpool Polytechnic in 1989, Burrell has participated in many group shows in Belfast (Old Museum, 1991; Ulster People's College, 1992; One Oxford Street, 1992; Flax Studios, 1992), in Derry and in Dublin (Head Gallery, 1994). She has also mounted two solo exhibitions in Belfast (in The Plaza 1993 and the Crescent Arts Centre 1992). Her work has received considerable media attention and has been reviewed in Circa, Gown Literary Supplement, The Irish News and The Irish Times. At present she lives and works in Belfast.

Elaine Callen

A founder member of Queen Street Studios, Callen lives and works in Belfast. She graduated from the University of Ulster in 1981, and has had many solo exhibitions in Northern Ireland (the Corridor Gallery, Lurgan 1987; Newry and Mourne Arts Centre, 1988; Lyric Theatre, Belfast 1989; Harmony Hill Arts Centre 1990). Her work has also been shown in numerous group exhibitions in Belfast as well as in London, Exeter, Dublin, Limerick, and Edinburgh.

Anne Clarke

Anne Clarke was a member of the management committee of Queen Street Studios and held the position of Treasurer from 1991 to 1992. Born in Derry, she attended the University of Ulster at Belfast where she was awarded a BA degree in 1985. Her solo exhibitions include "Transition" (Harmony Hill, Lisburn 1992); "Moondreaming Early Morning" Peacock, Craigavon (1990) and "Sense", Temple Court, Belfast (1993). Her work has also been shown as part of group exhibitions in the Old Museum and Crescent Arts Centres among others. She has held residencies at the Tyrone Gutherie Arts Centre, Annamakerrig (1993) and at the Sculpture Symposium, Waterford (1990). Active also in Education, Clarke has lectured in Belfast at the University of Ulster, and in Derry at the College of Technology and the Orchard Gallery.

Brian Connolly

A graduate of the University of Ulster at Belfast (BA, 1984; MA, 1985), Connolly is a multi media artist who has exhibited extensively on the international scene. His most recent commissioned sculpture, "Turning Point", is sited in St. Anne's Square, Belfast. An EV+A prizewinner and recipient of numerous awards from the Arts Council, Connolly has also lectured in Nova Scotia College of Art, Sheffield Polytechnic, University of Ulster, the Colleges of Art in Cork and Limerick and Queen's University. He is on the editorial board of Circa, and has instigated and organised a number of significant arts events including "Available Resources" (Derry 1991) and "Random Access" (IMMA 1992).

Damien Coyle

Coyle was one of the founder members of the Queen Street Studio scheme in 1984. Born in Dungannon, he attended the University of Ulster where he was awarded a BA in Fine Art in 1981 and an MA in 1982. A regular contributor to Circa, Coyle was invited to join the editorial panel in 1993. His work has been shown extensively throughout Ireland as well as New York and Amsterdam. He has participated in the "Independent Artists" exhibition in the Douglas Hyde Gallery (1984). "Irish Exhibition of Living Art" in the Project Arts Centre (1985), and in a three person show at the Arts Council Gallery, Belfast (1993).

Marie Thérèse Davis

Davis graduated from Queen's University, Belfast with a BA in Social Anthropology in 1986. Having completed her post-graduate certificate in Education also at Queen's (1987), she then went on to study at the Oxford Polytechnic where she obtained a Certificate in Art and Design in 1990. She has worked as Visiting Artist in a Young Offenders Institution in Oxfordshire (1990), Visiting Lecturer in the Printmaking department of the Oxford Polytechnic and as a music teacher. Her work has featured in the AIB Better Ireland Awards on RTE2 (1993). Solo shows include "New Works", Flowerfield Arts Centre (1994); "Old Heads, Young Shoulders", Down Arts Centre (1994); "Drawings", Harmony Hill Arts Centre (1994).

Gerry Devlin

Having been awarded both a BA and the Advanced Diploma in Painting at the University of Ulster at Belfast (1977 and 1978), Devlin received the Ford Foundation Grant and went to study at Syracuse University, New York where he obtained a MFA in 1981. A prizewinner at the Claremorris Open Exhibition (1987 + 1994) and at "Works on Paper" at the Fenderesky Gallery (1988), Devlin's work has been shown at the Oireachtas Exhibition (1986), the "Independents '86" Exhibition in the Guinness Hop Store Dublin, and EV+A. He has had solo exhibitions in the Project Arts Centre, Dublin, the Garter Lane Arts Centre, Waterford and the Crawford Municipal Art Gallery, Cork (1990). He was invited to contribute to the "Great Book of Ireland", a work on Vellum, which was shown in IMMA and the Ulster Museum, Belfast, in 1991. His teaching experience includes that of Painting and Drawing tutor at the Crescent Arts Centre and the Workers Educational Association, Belfast; and also that of visiting Lecturer at the Dublin, Cork, Waterford, and Belfast Colleges of Art. Devlin has also been Artist in Residence for the Artists in Prisons Scheme, Dublin.

Moira Doherty

A graduate of the University of Ulster at Belfast (BA in Fine Art 1985), Doherty's work has been selected for the Claremorris Open Exhibition and the Annual Independent Artists Exhibition at the Arts Council, Belfast and the Guinness Hop Store (1985). She contributes to the education of disabled young people, and has undertaken the supervision of mural painting and drama workshops with a number of groups. The work produced has received many awards, (including the First Prize Barclay's Youth Award) and has been displayed and performed at selected public venues throughout Northern Ireland.

Micky Donnelly

Having studied at the University of Ulster at Belfast and been awarded the BA (1979) and the MA (1981) in Fine Art, Donnelly received the Arts Council of Northern Ireland Scholarship at the British School at Rome in 1985. He has had numerous one person exhibitions in Ireland and abroad, the most significant of which include: The Fenderesky Gallery (1984, 1990, 1993); The Arts Council Gallery (1987); the Third Eye Centre Glasgow (1988); The Galerie + Edition CAOC Berlin (1993); The Orchard Gallery Derry (1987 and 1992); The Taylor Galleries Dublin (1988 and 1992); The Anderson O'Day Gallery London (1991) and the Kultur Raum Milbertshofen Munich (1993). Donnelly's work has been selected for the majority of recent major Irish exhibitions which travelled abroad, among them: "Irish Art Now", Turin 1986; "Cries and Whispers", touring Australia and New Zealand 1988; "Selected Images", Riverside Studio London, 1988; "Germany/Ireland Exchange", touring Ireland and West Germany 1988-1989; "On the Balcony of the Nation", touring the USA 1990-1992; "The Fifth Province", touring Canada 1991-1993. A past member of the editorial board of Circa, Donnelly has written and lectured extensively on art. His work has been bought for many public collections including those of the Ulster Museum, the Arts Councils of Great Britain, Northern Ireland and the Republic of Ireland, the British Council, The European Parliament, Allied Irish Banks, and Guinness Peat Aviation.

Frank Eyre

Eyre graduated from the University of Ulster at Belfast in 1989, and at present is studying there for his MA degree. In the interim, he has had two solo exhibitions (One Oxford Street, Belfast 1992; Rubicon Gallery, Dublin, 1990), and has taken part in several group shows in Northern and Southern Ireland.

James Fearon

Fearon studied Fine Art at the University of Ulster at Belfast where he completed his BA degree in 1984. Since then he has had several solo exhibitions in Belfast (Orpheus Building 1990; Kerlin Gallery 1988; Crescent Arts Centre 1986). His "Scrolls" has been exhibited at a number of venues throughout Canada (Montreal, Saskatchewan, Alberta, Vancouver) in 1989-1990. Most recently (1993) his "Drawing for an Inner Room" has been shown in the New Plaza, Belfast and he has shown at the Mall Galleries London. He has participated in numerous group exhibitions in Northern Ireland and the Republic of Ireland as well as in Poland and London. In 1989 Fearon was invited to take up a residency at the Banff Arts Centre in Canada and in 1992, he took part in a Belfast/Berlin Exchange, and was funded by Aer Lingus and the Arts Council of Northern Ireland.

Paul Finnegan

A founder member of the Artists' Collective of Northern Ireland and the Queen Street Studios, Finnegan has exhibited extensively throughout Ireland. The venues for his solo shows include the Crescent Arts Centre, Belfast (1983); Fenderesky Gallery (1984); Art Advice Gallery (1989). His "Head to Head" was shown at Zakks Barbers Shop in Belfast in 1990. He has been invited to show in numerous prestigious exhibitions, among them the "Independent Artists", Douglas Hyde Gallery (1983); EV+A (1984); Royal Ulster Academy Exhibition, Ulster Museum (1986); Oireachtas (1986). Finnegan's work has also been selected for exhibitions in France, Scotland and England. A graduate of the University of Ulster (1981), he lives and works in Belfast.

George Fleming

Having worked in the Royal Navy and the British Merchant Navy for a number of years Fleming became a student in the University of Ulster at Belfast in 1987. Having graduated with a BA in Fine Art in 1991, he went on to complete a post graduate Diploma in Applied Arts in 1992. His work has been selected for numerous group exhibitions in Belfast, among them, the Arts Council Gallery (1988); Ulster Folk and Transport Museum (1990); and has also been shown in the United States (Texas, 1989; Indiana, 1992), and in Britain. His solo exhibition "Echoes" travelled throughout Northern Ireland in 1993 and 1994 and was the subject of an Educational film sponsored by the Cultural Traditions Group. Fleming has given many lectures to such bodies as the Northern Ireland Patchwork Guild, the Quilt Art Workshops and the University of Ulster at Belfast. He has also run workshops in the Ulster Folk and Transport Museum, Harmony Hill Arts Centre and the Arts and Crafts Gallery (Slane). He lives and works in Belfast.

Nora Gaston

Nora Gaston began her studies at the Belfast College of Art where she obtained a National Diploma in Design, Painting and Printing (1964). Subsequently she attended the University of New Brunswick in Canada where she graduated in 1979 with a B. Ed. She acted as Arts Adviser for the School Board in New Brunswick before taking up the post of Head of Printmaking and Surface Design in the New Brunswick Craft School in Fredericton (1982). She was a founder member of "Gallery Connection" Studios there (1984-1987). She then moved to Saudi Arabia where she worked as an Arts Consultant and as Adviser to the Falcon Fine Art Gallery in Riyadh. In 1990 Gaston was appointed to the Visual Arts Committee of the Arts Council (Northern Ireland). She has had numerous solo exhibitions which have been shown in Riyadh (1989+1990); in the University of Maine USA (1988+1994); The University of New Brunswick, (1987); and St Andrews, Canada (1986+1987). She has been invited to partake in many group exhibitions the most recent of which have taken place in the Arts Council Gallery in Belfast (1989, 1991, 1994). She has been commissioned to make stained glass windows for a Church in New Maryland (1982) and for a hospital in Fredericton, New Brunswick (1984), and to make a mural for Musgrave Park Hospital (1992). In 1987 Gaston's "With Bright Wings Hovering Over the Whole Earth" was selected for Exhibition at the United Nations Building in New York to mark the Year of Peace. At present she lives and works in Belfast.

Gerry Gleason

A founder member of Queen Street Studios, Gleason began his art career in 1976. His work has been selected for a number of group exhibitions, among them "Directions Out" which was shown in the Douglas Hyde Gallery in 1987 and "Parable Ireland" which took place in the Bluecoat Gallery Liverpool in 1991. Gleason has given solo exhibitions in the Orchard Gallery, Derry; The Arts Council Gallery, Edinburgh and the Galeria + Edition CAOC, in Berlin. His work has been bought by Derry City Council, the McLaurin Art Gallery, the Schloss Fredenstein Museen, Der Stadt Gotha and the Buchenwald Museum.

Nuala Gregory

Nuala Gregory joined the University of Ulster at Belfast in 1984 and graduated in 1988 with a First Class BA in Fine Art. She has recently been commissioned by the Arts Council of Northern Ireland to make a large screen for their offices in Riddell Hall, Belfast. Her solo exhibitions include "Recent Work" (1989-1990) which was shown in the Arts Council Gallery Window, Belfast and "Works on Paper" (1990) in the Peacock Gallery, Craigavon. Her work has been selected for the Claremorris Open Exhibition (1990); the Open Drawing Competition in the Old Museum Arts Centre (1990); Belfast Young Contemporaries in One Gallery (1992), and the Monaghan Open Exhibition (1993). She has participated in numerous group exhibitions in Northern Ireland and has been extensively reviewed in the National Press and Circa. Gregory has lectured in the University of Ulster and has run many workshops. She is listed on the Arts Council Lecturers and Readers Scheme.

Ian Hamilton

Ian Hamilton attended Manchester Art College, graduating in 1987 with a BA in Fine Art. He has had several solo exhibitions; Lyric Theatre Belfast (1989), Project Art Centre, Dublin (1990), Navan Arts Festival (1990) and the Kerlin Gallery, Belfast (1990). He has participated also in group shows in the Fenderesky Gallery (1988), the Belltable, Limerick (1990) and One Oxford Street Gallery, Belfast (1992+1993). His work has been selected for the "BP Young European Artists", shown in Brussels in 1991 and the "Belfast Young Contempories" shown in Belfast and London in 1992. Hamilton lives and works in Galway and Co. Down.

John Hamilton

Having worked for a number of years in the Civil Service, Hamilton came to the University of Ulster at Belfast in 1980 from where he graduated with a BA in Fine Art in 1984. The following year he showed in Queen Street, as well as in the "On the Wall Young Artists" group show, and the Alternative Lifestyles bookshop in Belfast. He also took part in a two person exhibition in the Otter Gallery, Belfast in that year. In the interim his work has been exhibited in the Harmony Hill Arts Centre (1986+1989) and in the Crescent Arts Centre (1989).

Kathy Herbert

Kathy Herbert graduated from the University of Ulster with a BA in Fine Art in 1990, having transferred from the National College of Art and Design, Dublin where she spent three years. Her sculpture has been selected for many significant Symposia among them, The Castlewellan Forest Park Sculpture Symposium (1992); The Snow Sculpture Symposium, Luleå Sweden (1992); The Boglands Symposium Co. Wicklow (1990). She was a prizewinner at the "Íontas" Small Works Competition in Sligo in 1991. She has also been invited to show at the Crescent Arts Centre's Exhibition "The Human Form" (1993); "Random Access" at the Irish Life Mall, Dublin (1993); The Oireachtas Exhibition, RHA Gallery, Dublin (1993); The "Boglands" Exhibition, Crescent Arts Centre, Belfast (1990) and Irish Life Mall, Dublin, (1991); and the "New Artists" Exhibition in Fenderesky Gallery at Queen's (1991). Herbert was the Artist in Residence in St. Patrick's College, Dublin in 1992 and has worked for some years as a tutor for the Adult Life Drawing Class at the Crescent Arts Centre and the Royal Ulster Academy Association, Belfast.

Frank Holmes

Since his graduation (BA in Fine Art, University of Ulster at Belfast, 1990) Holmes has participated in numerous group exhibitions in Belfast and the environs. He also participated in the Belfast/Berlin Exchange and the Belfast/Bristol Exchange in 1992. He has also organised and run numerous workshops at: The East Belfast Festival (1991); The Dale Farm Library (1991-1992), The Adventure Playground, Berlin (1992) and at Queen Street Studios (1993). Holmes has also taught at St. Mary's Training College (1991) and at Dunmurry High School (1991-1992).

Ronnie Hughes

Hughes studied at the University of Ulster at Belfast where he was awarded a First Class BA in 1988, and an MA in Fine Art in 1989. His solo exhibitions include: "Open Studio", PS1 Museum, New York (1991); "Emigrant Landscape", Rubicon Gallery, Dublin (1991) and Belfast Arts Council Gallery (1992); "Consummation", Orpheus Gallery, Belfast (1992); "City Reformed", Rubicon Gallery, Dublin and Limerick City Gallery of Art (1993). His work has been selected for exhibition at EV+A in 1990, 1992 and 1993; and for the Claremorris Open Exhibition in 1989 and 1992. Hughes has also been shown at the Fenderesky Gallery (1992+1993) and the Barbican Gallery, London (1992). He is the recipient of the first prize at the Taylor Awards (1989). His work has been extensively reviewed in the National Press and Circa, and forms part of the collection of Ark Life Assurance; the Arts Council of Northern Ireland; BP Oil, Europe; Irish Contemporary Arts Society and Monaghan County Museum.

Tim Johnson

Born in Newcastle-Upon-Tyne, Johnson studied painting, photography, sculpture and installation at Reading University from where he graduated in 1989. He moved to Ireland in 1990, and has exhibited throughout Ireland in the interim. His work has most recently been shown at the Pan Celtic Arts Festival, Galway; the Ulster Arts Club, Belfast, the Donegal County Museum, Letterkenny and at the Irish Wild Bird Conservancy's Twenty-Fifth Anniversary Exhibition at the Bank of Ireland Arts Centre, Dublin.

Barbara Lavery

Having completed the Foundation Certificate in Art and Design at the University of Ulster at Belfast (1988), Barbara Lavery went to Newcastle-Upon-Tyne Polytechnic where she was awarded a BA Degree in Fine Art (1991). In 1994 she received her MA (Fine Art) from Birmingham Institute of Art and Design. Her work has been shown in Newcastle (1989, 1990); in Durham (1991) and London (1991). More recently she participated in "No Access", Ross's Court Belfast (1992); "House Spirit" in Gheister House Berlin (1992) and "Vessels", Eagle Works Gallery, Wolverhampton (1994). In 1992 Lavery took part in the Belfast/Berlin Artist Exchange Project and she has also organised and conducted workshops in Newcastle and in Belfast. In 1993 she received the Great Britain and Northern Ireland Humanities Bursary.

Colette Lee

In 1983 Collette Lee joined the Great Yarmouth College of Art and Design, where she qualified with a BTEC Diploma in 1985. She then moved to the Gloucestershire College of Art and Technology from where she graduated with a BA degree in Fine Art in 1988. In 1989 she was awarded an MA by the University of Ulster at Belfast. She was commissioned by Gloucestershire County Council to make a Bronze Plaque (1989), and by the Plaza Hotel, Belfast to make a Sculpture (1990). Her work has been shown in Cheltenham (1987), Gloucestershire (1988), Slaughterhouse Gallery, London and the ILAC Centre, Dublin (1989). Lee also took part in the "No Access" Exhibition (1992); in a group exhibition at the Gallerie Hausgeist, Berlin (1992); and the "Young Contemporaries" One Oxford Street, Belfast (1993). At present she is working towards a Group Show at the Issus Gallery in Cumbria to be shown in October 1994.

Terry McAllister

A recent Graduate of the University of Ulster at Belfast (BA in Fine Art, 1990), McAllister's work has been shown throughout Northern Ireland. His first solo exhibition was held in the New Plaza, Belfast in 1994, and he holds the Silver Medal awarded by the Royal Ulster Academy in 1990. He was selected for the Claremorris Open Competition also in that year. In 1992 he took part in a Slide Presentation with three colleagues and members of "Voices Northern Ireland" which was held at five venues in Belfast, and also participated in the "No Access" group show at the Belfast Youth and Community Centre. He took part in "Trasna", a Belfast/Glasgow Exchange in 1993, and his work was exhibited in the Transmission Gallery, Glasgow.

Colin McGookin

Colin McGookin is a founder member of both the Artists' Collective of Northern Ireland and Queen Street Studios and has served as Northern Ireland representative to the Artists' Association of Ireland (1988-1991) and Board member of the Crescent Arts Centre (1993-1994). He graduated from the Ulster College of Art (BA 1981) and has since exhibited extensively throughout Ireland, Britain and the Continent. His solo exhibitions include "Distant Woodworks" (touring Northern Ireland 1993-1994); "Scene from the Projection Box" (Orchard Gallery 1992); "Divided Society"(McLaurin Art Gallery, Ayr 1992); "From Tradition into the Light" (touring throughout Ireland 1991); and "Collaborators" (Arts Council Gallery Belfast and National Poetry Society, London 1989). He has been invited to show in many prestigious exhibitions of Irish Art: "Directions Out" (Douglas Hyde Gallery, Dublin 1987); "Parable Island" (Bluecoat Gallery Liverpool 1991); "In a State" (Kilmainham Gaol, Dublin 1991) to name but a few. Other group shows in Ireland and abroad include "Irish Exhibition of Living Art" (1980 + 1981); "Independent Artists" (1985 + 1986); EV+A (1986); Royal Ulster Academy (1986,1987,1989,1991,1993); Claremorris Open (1986, 1987, 1989, 1990, 1991, 1993) where he was a prizewinner in 1990; "Exchange" (Hull 1986); "Four Belfast Artists" (Exmouth 86); "Four Painters" (Stranraer 1987); "Europe's Landscapes" (Albert, France 1993); "Mail Bang" (Helsinki, 1993). His work features in many public and private collections and has been reviewed extensively in the National Press. He has received many prizes and awards including Arts Council of Northern Ireland Bursaries (1992 + 1993) and is an elected Associate Member of Royal Ulster Academy since 1989. Currently employed by Lisburn Borough Council as an arts worker, McGookin lives and works in Belfast.

Jim McKevitt

A graduate of the University of Ulster at Belfast, McKevitt's work has been shown extensively throughout Northern Ireland and Europe. Most recently he has been selected to appear in "New Artists" (Fenderesky Gallery Belfast 1991) "New Contemporaries" (One Oxford Street, Belfast and London 1992 and 1993). He has also exhibited in Edinburgh (Ash Gallery 1991); in Germany (Galerie Martin Schmitz, Kassel 1992, Galerie Pigment, Kassel 1993, Galerie + Edition CAOC, Berlin 1991 + 1992): and in Poland (Baltic Art Gallery Uskta 1993 + 1994). His work was featured in "I am History Now" (1993), a touring exhibition which is being shown at a number of venues in Northern Ireland before travelling to the Itami Museum of Contemporary Culture in Japan. McKevitt lives in Belfast and works in Queen Street Studios.

John Mathers

Following his graduation from the University of Ulster at Belfast (BA in Fine Art 1988), Mathers had several solo exhibitions (Omagh Tourist and Information Centre 1989; Harmony Hill Arts Centre, 1991). His work has been selected for many group exhibitions, the most recent of which are the "Artists' Collective Open Exhibition", Laganside Galleries Belfast (1990); "Group Show" One Oxford Street Gallery (1991); "Four Belfast Artists" Artspace Gallery Bristol (1992); "No Access", The Plaza, Belfast (1992) and "Still Lives" an Arts Council Touring Exhibition (1993). In 1994 Mathers participated in a two person show at the Arts Council Gallery, Belfast. In 1990 he travelled throughout the USA where he studied the work of Edward Hopper as well as visiting the major collections in the East and West Coast Galleries. He also spent a five week residency at the Bristol Artspace Studios (1992).

Michael Minnis

In 1986 Michael Minnis graduated with a First Class BA (Painting) from Manchester Polytechnic and in 1989 he was awarded an MA in Fine Art by the University of Ulster at Belfast. He is the co-founder and Secretary of the FlaxArt Studios, Belfast where he is currently working. His work has been selected to be shown in numerous exhibitions, among them EV+A (1991, 1992, and 1993); "See Through Art" in the Municipal Art Gallery, Dublin (1993); "Shifting Borders" commissioned by the Laing Art Gallery as part of a European Arts Festival (1992). Minnis has also participated in several touring exhibitions such as the "British Telecom New Contemporaries" (1989-1990); "Shocks to the System" (1991-1992) both of which travelled to many galleries in Britain. He received the Prince's Trust Award in 1990, and in 1993 he also received the Victor Treacy Award at the Butler Gallery Kilkenny. In that year he was invited to mount a solo exhibition in the Werkstatt Galerie in Bremen, Germany.

Alfonso López Monreal

Born in Mexico, Monreal spent seven years as a student of the Guanajuato University in his country, after which he moved to "Atelier 17" in Paris in 1976. He lectured in printmaking in Barcelona (1978-79), in the National College of Art and Design, Dublin (1987-88) and in the University of Ulster at Belfast (1988-89). Having studied advanced techniques of restoration, Monreal was appointed as Director of Restoration for the Musea Pedro Coronel in Zacatecas, Mexico in 1981, where he also lectured in Fine Art. From 1990 onwards, however, he has worked only as a full-time artist. His solo exhibitions are too numerous to list. Suffice to say that they have taken place in venues in Mexico (1974, 1979, 1980, 1982, 1991, 1992 and 1993); in Barcelona (1978, 1981, 1982); in Belfast (Fenderesky Gallery 1984, 1985, 1987, 1990; Arts Council Gallery, 1987 and 1992); in Dublin (Taylor Galleries 1987, 1988, 1991, 1993); and in Derry (Orchard Gallery, 1992). His work was selected for the Chicago International "Art Expo" in 1994. In the previous year he had also presented a solo exhibition at the Prospectus Gallery in Chicago. Monreal has won a number of major prizes at the open competitions both in Mexico and Ireland and he has also received many significant commissions for murals and prints in both countries.

Amanda Montgomery

Having completed her Foundation course at the University of Ulster at Belfast, Amanda Montgomery moved to Coventry where she studied at the School of Art and Design at Coventry University. In 1991 she graduated with a BA (First Class) in Fine Art. Her solo exhibitions include "Sense..." which was shown in the Ardhowen Theatre in Enniskillen and in the Crescent Arts Centre in 1993. She has also been represented in many group exhibitions, among them the "Whitefriars Sculpture Exhibition" Coventry (1990 + 1991); the "Fresh Art Fair" in Islington, London (1991); "No Access" at Ross's Court Belfast (1992) and the "Dunchurche Sculpture Park" Touring Exhibition Warwickshire (1993 and 1994). Montgomery has taught on the Sculpture course in the University of Ulster at Belfast (1992). She was the Artist in Residence at the Share Centre for disabled and able bodied in Co. Fermanagh (1992-1993).

Deirdre O'Connell

Deirdre O'Connell graduated with a First Class honours BA Degree from the North Staffordshire Polytechnic in Stoke-on-Trent in 1978, and went on to study at the University of Ulster at Belfast where she was awarded an MA in Fine Art in 1980. At present she is working on three solo exhibitions, all planned for the current year (Fenderesky, Belfast; Studio Bocchi, Rome; Orchard Gallery, Derry). She has had several solo exhibitions in venues throughout Northern Ireland including her "Insula Penninsula" (Arts Council Gallery, Belfast, 1990); has been selected for a number of Open Shows (Claremorris, 1985, 1990; EV+A 1985); as well as being represented in the "Irish Exhibition of Living Art" (Guinness Hop Store, 1985); "The New Tradition" (Douglas Hyde, 1991); "Artae" (Ferrara and Rome, 1991); "The Fifth Province" (Edmonton Art Gallery and Touring Canada, 1991- 1993) "Human Properties" Ikon Gallery, Birmingham, 1992); "Encounters with Diversity" (PS1 Museum, New York, 1992); "Fields of Vision" (Trout Gallery, Carlisle, Pennsylvania, 1993). In 1991 O'Connell won the Studio Scholarship for the PS1 Studio Residency in New York. She is a regular contributor to Circa and was a member of the Editorial Panel. She has also taught and lectured extensively at Colleges of Art in Ireland and Britain.

Eleanor O'Donovan

Eleanor O'Donovan studied at the College of Art in Limerick where she completed a Certificate Course in Visual Education in 1987. She then moved to the University of Ulster at Belfast from where she graduated in 1990 with a BA Degree in Fine Art. In 1991 she was invited to take up a Residency in Langholm Studios, Ayrshire in Scotland. She has been represented at many group exhibitions in both the North and South of Ireland, for example, her work was included in "That's a Good Question" and "That's Another Good Question" (Harmony Hill Arts Centre 1989 and 1990); "No Access" (Ross's Court, 1992); "Lifescapes" (Harmony Hill Arts Centre, 1993). She was selected for the Monaghan Open Exhibition in 1993, and has been commissioned to make a sculpture ("Talking North") for Liverpool (1991).

Tony Ó Gribín

Born in Belfast, Ó Gribín completed his Foundation Course at the Ulster Polytechnic at Jordanstown in 1975. He went on to study at the Exeter College of Art where he graduated with a BA Degree in Fine Art in 1978. He has worked abroad for many years. In 1978 he travelled to Paris where he lived for a year and in 1981 he worked in West Germany for an extended period. He has been represented in numerous group shows in Ireland and Britain, and his work is included in many private collections in Ireland, Germany, Britain, Spain and the USA.

Jack Pakenham

Pakenham graduated from Queen's University Belfast in 1959 with a Degree in French, Spanish and Philosophy. He then moved to Ibiza where he spent some time writing and painting. A teacher of English Literature for many years, Pakenham is himself a writer as well as a painter and has had several collections of poetry published. ("Spent the Morning", 1974; "Who Will Tell Them?", 1976; "The Last Day", 1980). He has had numerous solo exhibitions from 1960 onwards. Among the more recent have been "A Broken Sky" 1990, (Orchard Gallery, Derry and Project Gallery, Dublin); "Selected Work" 1991,(Wyvern Gallery, Dublin); "Die Strasse Explodiert in Meinen Kopf" 1992 (Galerie + Edition CAOC and front* Art, Berlin). He has been invited to mount numerous solo exhibitions: Fenderesky (1984, 1988, 1991); Hendricks (1987); Tom Caldwell (1972, 1975, 1981); and has been represented in countless group shows in Ireland, England, Scotland, Germany and Canada. The recipient of a number of prestigious awards and commissions, Pakenham has been extensively reviewed in the National Press and Circa by John Hutchinson (1987) and Dr. S. Sverakova (1990). In 1987 he was elected an Academician by the Royal Ulster Academy.

Mark Pepper

Graduating in 1985 from the University of Ulster at Belfast, Pepper then went on to be awarded the MA in Fine Art from that University in 1986. In 1984 he was a prizewinner in the Guinness Peat Aviation Awards for Emerging Artists, and his work was on exhibition at the RHA Gallery in Dublin. In 1985 he was selected for the Claremorris Open Competition, (where he was also a prizewinner), and for EV+A in Limerick. He was represented at a number of exhibitions in the North and South of Ireland, among them "Six Artists" (Foyle Project, Derry 1986); "On the Go" (Temple Bar Dublin 1987); "Artists Endeavour" (Otter Gallery Belfast 1987); "Springboard" (Irish Life Exhibition Centre, Dublin, 1990) and "Gateway to Art" (Aer Rianta Arts Festival, Dublin Airport 1993). His work has also been included in Exhibitions in the Arts Council Gallery, Belfast (1988 + 1992) and at the Orchard Gallery, Derry (1993).

Robert Peters

Peters is a Co-Initiator and Director of "Catalyst Arts", a dynamic artists' collaborative active in setting up exhibitions, workshops, seminars and lectures which was inaugurated in Belfast late in 1993. In 1992 he set up and organised the Rudolf Steiner Teachers Conference in Hollywood, Co. Down. He contributes to the education of students at this college in the areas of both Art and Drama. Peters has been commissioned to paint several large murals for the private and public sector. His murals can be seen in the Harland and Wolff Welders Club, (1986); The Royal Victoria Hospital (1987 + 1990); Craigavon Hospital (1988) and Hilltown P.S. (1989). A graduate of the University of Ulster at Belfast (BA in Fine Art 1984) Peters has been invited to partake in several group exhibitions including the Crescent Arts Centre, 1985. Also in that year he had a solo exhibition in the Crescent, and his work was selected for "Irish Living Arts" in the Guinness Hop Store in Dublin. He has also shown in the Belfast Film Workshop (1985/86).

Simon Reilly

Born in Dublin, Simon Reilly began his studies in the College of Marketing and Design in Parnell Square, where he completed his Foundation Course in 1979. He then moved to the University of Ulster at Belfast where he graduated with a BA in Fine Art in 1985. He has had several solo exhibitions in galleries of note such as The Project Arts Centre, Dublin (1986); The Arts Council Gallery, Belfast (1988 and 1992); The Kerlin Gallery Belfast (1989) and Temple Bar Gallery, Dublin (1992). In 1989 Reilly won the Arts Council Scholarship to the British School in Rome where he spent a year. His work was shown there and subsequently was chosen for representation at the "Ten years of the British School in Rome" Exhibition in London (1990). He has taken part in numerous group Exhibitions in the North and South of Ireland as well as in Berlin (BAUH 5, 1990); Geneva ("Nothing to Declare", 1994) and in Tokyo at the New Museum of Contemporary Art in 1994.

Nicola Russell

Having completed the Foundation Course at the University of Ulster at Belfast in 1983, Nicola Russell studied at the Winchester School of Art in Hampshire, where she was awarded a BA in Fine Art in 1986. Her solo exhibitions include "Rose Series" shown at the Fenderesky Gallery, Belfast in 1989; "Gyn-Ecological Drawings" at the Crescent Arts Centre in Belfast in 1993; "Gathering of Opposites" at the Arts Council Gallery in Belfast in 1993; and "New Work" at the Orchard Gallery, Derry also in 1993. She is represented in "Still Lives", a travelling group exhibition sponsored by the Arts Council of Northern Ireland (1993). Russell won the Fellowship to the British School in Rome for 1993-1994 and her work was exhibited there in 1994. She took part in "Hausegeist/Nomade" a Berlin Exchange Scheme in 1992. She has participated in numerous group exhibitions of note, among them "Art Endeavours" (1988) Otter Gallery, Belfast and the National Institute of Higher Education, Limerick; "Collective Images" (1990) Laganside Gallery, Belfast; "Drawing Exhibition" (1991) Old Museum Arts Centre, Belfast; "Art Lovers" (1992) Crawford Gallery, Cork. Her work has been included at exhibitions in the Fenderesky Gallery, Belfast (1989) and the Arts Council Gallery, Belfast (1992).

Dermot Seymour

Born in Belfast, Seymour graduated from the University of Ulster in 1978 (BA in Fine Art) and received his Advanced Diploma in 1981 from the same University. He has exhibited extensively on the international scene and his one person shows include Art and Research Exchange Belfast (1978 and 1981); Fenderesky Gallery at Queen's Belfast (1986); Paula Allen Gallery, New York (1987, 1988, 1989); Arts Council Gallery Belfast (1989) and Pentonville Gallery London (1988). He has been invited to participate in many group shows: "Clean Irish Sea" (exhibition touring Ireland and UK 1989); "Irish Artists Working in New York" (USA 1988); "GPA Exhibition of Ulster Art" (Dublin 1988); PS1 Museum (New York 1988); Amos Anderson Museum (Helsinki 1988); "State of the Nation" (Coventry 1987); "Directions Out" (Dublin 1987); Fenderesky Gallery at Queen's (Belfast 1987); GPA Emerging Artists (Dublin 1986); "Independent Artists" (Dublin, Limerick, Belfast 1986 + 1985); "Divisions, Crossroads, Turns of Mind" (touring USA, Canada, Dublin and Finland 1985-1987). Seymour's work has been reviewed by International and National Press and Art Publications: Artforum, Circa, New York Observer, Art Monthly, Guardian, Le Soliel Quebec, Irish Times, RTE and BBC. The Arts Council of Northern Ireland and An Chomhairle Ealaíon, the Claremorris Open and the Department of Foreign Affairs in Dublin are among his awards. He currently lives and works in Co. Mayo.

Derek Smith

Derek Smith studied at the University of Ulster at Belfast, graduating in 1989 with a BA in Fine Art. Since then he has had several solo exhibitions including a Window Exhibition at the Arts Council Gallery, Belfast (1991); "1000 Candles" at the Tyrone Gutherie Centre in Monaghan (1991). In 1992 he had two solo exhibitions of his Drawings, Prints and Sculpture in Quebec, Canada (Centre D'Exposition, and L'Atelier les Milles Feuilles); and he also participated in two Snow Sculpture Events in Quebec in that year, as well as being represented at the International Biennale Print Exhibition there. He has also shown extensively in Belfast in a number of galleries including the Old Museum Arts Centre, Harmony Hill Arts Centre, the Laganside Gallery (1990) and the Octagon Gallery (1987). In 1987 Smith took part in an Exchange Print Exhibition with the University of China.

Nick Stewart

Nick Stewart studied Biology and Environmental Science at the University of Ulster at Jordanstown between 1970 and 1974, and subsequently attended the Belfast College of Art and Design where he was awarded a BA in Fine Art in 1981. At present he is living in Sheffield where he works as an artist and as a tutor at the Sheffield Polytechnic. Stewart has received many prizes and bursaries of note including those of the "Irish Exhibition of Living Art" (1985, 1987); "The Projects UK" Bursary for commissioned performance work (1986); the Hull Time Based Bursary to present site specific work (1989) and for the Thorne Moors Project (1993); The Canada Council Bursary, for a Residency at the Articule Gallery, Montreal (1989); The Irish Arts Council Bursary for commissioned Installation work for "Diaspora" (1993); to name but a few. He has presented numerous exhibitions of Performance, Installation and Video work as well as drawings in the USA, Canada, France, Italy, Ireland and Britain. He had also taught and lectured extensively at Colleges of Art, Universities and Galleries throughout Britain and Ireland, as well as contributing to Circa, Artists' Newsletter, Hybrid and Creative Camera.

Elaine Thompson

Elaine Thompson graduated from Edinburgh College of Art in 1992, with a BA in Painting and Drawing, and then went on to study at Windsor School of Art (MA in European Fine Art 1993). She has worked at Restoration in France, as an English Teacher in Spain (1993) and Corsica (1989) and has visited L'Ecole des Beaux Arts in Montpelier through the Erasumus Exchange Programme. As part of her MA programme, her studio was based in Barcelona from September 1992 - June 1993 and incorporated some time spent in Alaior, Menorca. She has exhibited her work in Barcelona (1993) and in Scotland (1992). She has also been the recipient of the Ulster Television Award for Young Artists (1991). Thompson is currently living in Belfast.

Hillary Tully

Having studied at the National College of Art and Design in Dublin (1986-1987) and the Limerick School of Art and Design (1987-1990) Tully moved to Belfast. Her solo shows "Fetish" and "Strata" were exhibited at the New Plaza Gallery, Belfast and the Newry and Mourne Arts Centre in 1993. Her work has been included in many group exhibitions including "Limerick Women Artists", Belltable Arts Centre, Limerick (1989); "Limerick Women Artists" Flag Gallery, Limerick (1990); "No Access" Crescent Arts Centre, Belfast and An Culturlann, Falls Road, Belfast (1992); "Grupa Gan Ainm" and "Féila Lúnasa", An Culturlann, Falls Road, Belfast (1993).

Martin Wedge

Wedge studied at the College of Art in Belfast where he graduated in 1980 with a BA in Fine Art. In 1981 he undertook further study and was awarded an MA in Fine Art in 1982. In 1985 he received an award from the Arts Council of Ireland to study with Sandro Chia in New York for a year. Wedge also worked as a studio assistant to Brian Wood in New York in 1986. He has given a number of Street Performances throughout Ireland, as well as presenting performance/installation work in Galleries; (Triskel Arts Centre, Cork 1992; UCC Boole Library, 1991; Crescent Arts Centre, Belfast 1982; College of Art, Belfast 1980-1981). His solo exhibitions have been held in the Triskel Arts Centre, Cork (1992); The Kerlin Gallery (1989); "On the Wall Gallery, Belfast, (1989); and the Octagon Gallery Belfast (1981). Wedge has been invited to partake in numerous Group Exhibitions, the most recent of which are: "The Human Form" (Crescent Arts Centre, Belfast, 1993); "Art of Works" (Arts Council Gallery, Belfast 1993); Group Exhibition at the Fenderesky Gallery (1993); "Images of Ourselves" (Triskel Arts Centre, Cork 1992 ands 1991); "Irish Contemporaries Exhibition" (Gallagher Gallery, Dublin 1991); "Strongholds" (Tate Gallery and touring to Finland 1991); "New North" (Tate Gallery and travelling to Laing Gallery Newcastle, Tramway Gallery Glasgow, Orchard Gallery Derry, and Mappin Gallery Sheffield, 1990-1991).

Chris Wilson

Having graduated from Brighton College of Art in 1982, Chris Wilson returned to his native Belfast where he became a founder member of the Queen Street Studios (1984). He worked in these Studios for three years, and describes the experience as "full of good memories and thoughts of a small group who made something work with little money and often in the face of an apathetic establishment". He first exhibited in Belfast as part of the "Collective Show" at Queen Street Studios. Since then he has been invited to participate in numerous exhibitions internationally (Ireland, Germany, Hong Kong and the USA). Wilson recently received a Bursary from the British Council in order to organise and show a solo exhibition in Romania (1992) and Bulgaria (1993).

Sally Young

Born in Belfast, Sally Young attended the University of Ulster at Belfast from where she graduated in 1991 with a BA in Fine Craft Design. Since then she has taken part in several exhibitions in Belfast (The "Opening Exhibition" and "No Access" in Ross's Court, 1991 and 1992; Aumonier Salon, 1992; Culturlann Gallery, Hugh Frew Gallery, and Crescent Arts Centre 1993). Young has also been invited to exhibit in the Geisterhaus Gallery, Berlin (1992) and the Irish Craft Exhibition in London (1991). She has received two awards from the Princes Trust, to wit a "Go And See" Grant in 1992, and an "In Pursuit of Excellence" Grant in 1993.

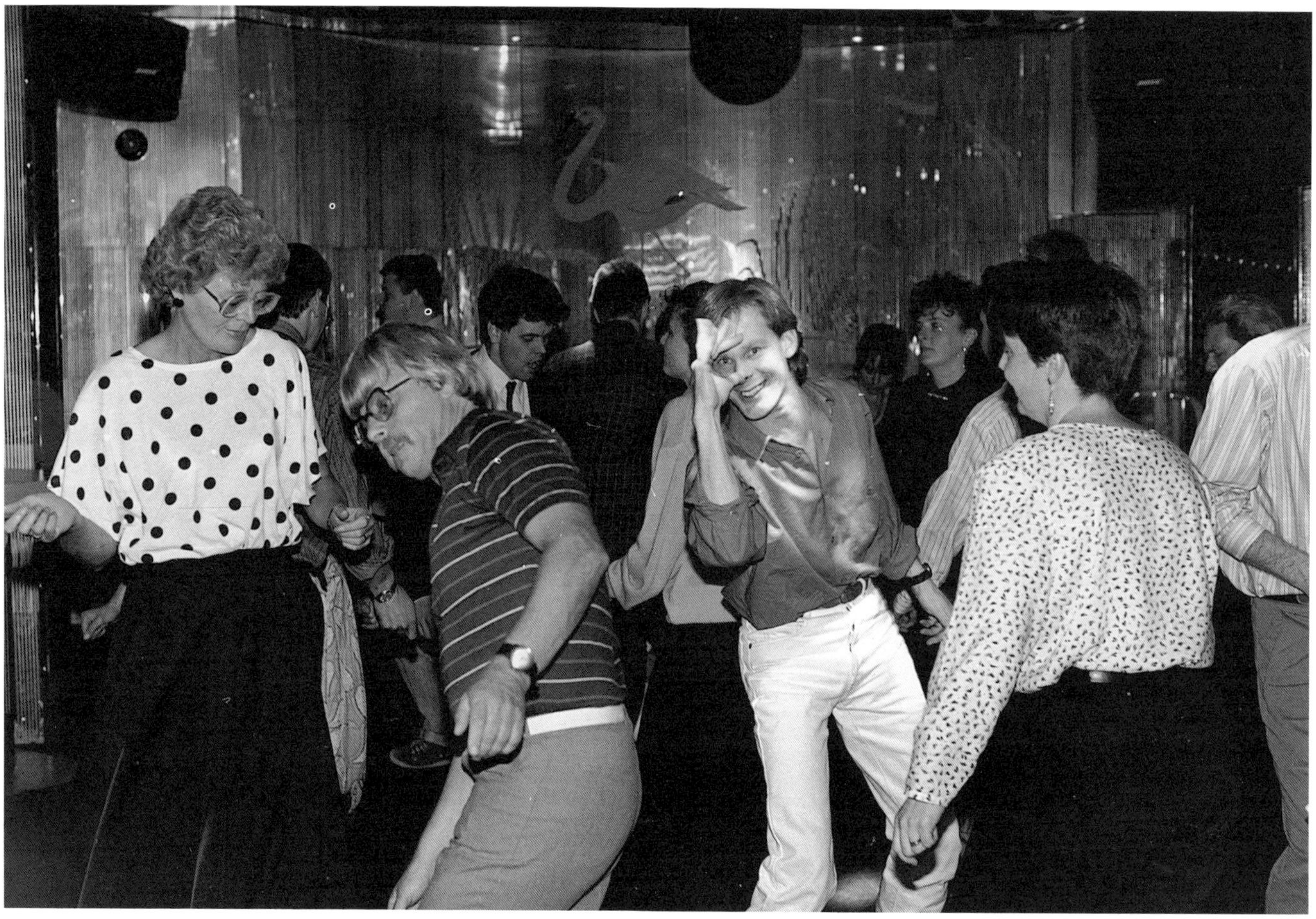